MW00800611

BAD
MEDICINE

Life prescriptions from M.D. Hirschberg

Addicted to Hope 2016

MATTHEW D. HIRSCHBERG

WITH JAY W. FOREMAN

Copyright © 2014 by Matthew D. Hirschberg

All rights reserved. No part of this publication may be reproduced, distributed, or transmitted in any form or by any means, including photocopying, recording, or other electronic or mechanical methods, without the prior written permission of the author, except in the case of brief quotations embodied in critical reviews and certain other noncommercial uses permitted by copyright law.

2

Disclaimer

While the content of this story is accurate to the best of my recollection, some names and locations have been changed and a few situations have been omitted completely. The reason for these modifications is as follows: The purpose of this book is to encourage and build up others, not to dispirit or tear anyone down. While I am comfortable sharing my story in its entirety, other reputations were protected. Please be assured that the revisions are minimal and in no way diminish the integrity of this biography.

Acknowledgements

This project would not have been possible without the support and encouragement of others. I would like to give a special thank you to them now.

Jay W. Foreman – Jay was my first choice for a writer to partner with on this project, so I was extremely excited when he agreed to come on board. I have read all of his books and thoroughly enjoy his writing style. Throughout this endeavor, Jay was able to accurately capture my personality and seamlessly inject it into the story. He helped to create a balance of the highlights and lowlights in my life that gave the story a fluent continuity. I encourage you to check out Jay's other books. He offers everything from children's stories to young adult novels to motivational and faith-based books for adults. You can learn more about Jay at **jaywforeman.com**.

Jeremy Wright – I consider Jeremy my best friend and my story would not have taken me to where I am today without his encouragement, support and loyalty. Between what he has taught me and the opportunities he has provided me, I am humbled and honored to have him in my life. While I will never be able to repay him for all he has done for me, I can definitely take a page out of his book and help others when and where I can. Jeremy is an inspiration and a role model, and I'm proud that he is a significant part of my life's journey. Jeremy is the founder and CEO of Body Renew Fitness in Winchester, Virginia. Check out the business at **bodyrenewwinchester.com**.

My Family – None of this would be possible without the unconditional love of my family. They have supported and stood by me from the beginning to where I am today. While I may not have always appreciated how special family can be, I do now. And I am thankful to have each and every one of them in my life.

Forward

Our lives are lived in layers. The veneer we see on someone's outer shelf today is not always backed by good wood underneath. As you engage in the layers of Matt's life, you will experience rotten wood made strong. I first met Matt as a troubled young man battling obesity, addiction and a quickly approaching prison sentence. When he walked into my office four years later I literally did not recognize him. He visited unannounced and introduced himself. I looked into the face of a physically fit, well-groomed, confident and articulate man. I greeted him as an old friend while my brain was in total shock of what stood before me. The only familiar association I could trace from when I knew Matt before was the distinction of his hands. I was looking at a total transformation! As you read, regardless of which "layer of life" you find yourself in, you will be encouraged! If you are a parent with a challenging son or daughter, you will find hope. If you are trapped in an addictive cycle, you will find answers. If you are feeling worthless or wonder whether you can ever change and add value to society, then *Bad Medicine* is a must read for you! The life prescriptions at the end, if followed, will extract the "bad medicine" from your life. I gleaned in reading that parents are the foundation regardless of how your children turn out. Matt always returned home, and knew he was welcomed. Second, your friends matter! The proverb claiming, "bad company corrupts good character" is true! And finally, you can always change! It starts when you decide. Matt's story will inspire young and old together. It conveys both a road to not travel, but also a clear path back if you made the wrong turn. Matt, I'm proud of you for being an inspiration to others as well as an example to follow!

Pastor Bobby Alger
Crossroads Community Church
crossroadswinchester.com

Chapter 1

My hands shook as I poured myself a glass of water. I tried my best to steady them, but failed. My forehead started to moisten from sweat. I was doing everything in my power to remain calm…or to at least look the part. But it wasn't working. I took a huge gulp of water and swallowed. I wasn't thirsty. I was simply trying to remedy the dry throat I had suddenly developed. Hands still shaking, I noisily set my glass back down on the stained mahogany table at which I was sitting.

And I wasn't alone. Across from me sat a United States Attorney. He hadn't taken his eyes off of me since I entered the room five minutes ago. It wasn't as if he were sizing me up either. He stared at me with a conviction that said he knew everything there was to know about me before I even sat down.

Flanked to his left and right sat representatives from the FBI, ATF, DEA and various other three-letter law enforcement agencies with which I was unfamiliar. But they all had one common bond that brought them to the table. The

United States Federal Government had utilized all of them to take me down. There was a time that I would have perceived this unsolicited attention as a compliment. But not now. This time felt different. More final.

I took a deep breath and exhaled, stretching my arms and placing the palms of my hands onto the cool hard table. My attorney, who was sitting next to me, placed his hand on my shoulder to let me know everything would be alright. And through his wordless gesture, I believed him. I had been in tight spots before. Heck, I'd been in life-threatening situations before. I'd outsmarted law enforcement in the past, and I could do it again. After all, I was a survivor. That's what I did. It's who I was.

Once the meeting started, the U.S. Attorney spoke at length as to why I was involuntarily summoned to join them on this day. When he was finally finished talking I felt like a knot had been tightened in the pit of my stomach. I looked to my attorney to see what our next move in this whole legal chess game was going to be. The expression on his face spoke volumes before he ever opened his mouth. He was stoic and slightly apologetic at the same time.

Then he spoke to me the two words that have stayed with me ever since.

"It's over."

And just like that...my life as I knew it truly was.

Chapter 2

That certainly wasn't my finest hour. In retrospect, it was one of the lowest points of my life. Little did I know that things would continue to get worse before they got better. Sit back, grab a drink and allow me to catch you up on how I came to be sitting across the table from our federal law enforcement's finest.

It all started on March 13, 1980 when my parents gave birth to a bouncing baby boy. You guessed it...me. My dad, Dr. Stanley Hirschberg, was a prominent plastic surgeon at the time, and my mom, Sande Hirschberg, worked as my father's office manager and later opened her own business. Eventually, our family expanded, and I was joined by two siblings: my sister Jen (four years younger), and my brother Nathan (eleven years younger). We grew up in the historic city of Winchester, Virginia, where my father would be the area's first plastic surgeon. I call Winchester historic because it was the most contested city during the Civil War. In fact, Winchester changed hands between the Union and the Confederacy more than seventy times.

We actually lived in a restored house dating back to the Civil War. It was a large two-story building with a white wood exterior offset by black shutters and red tin roof. A front porch complete with towering white pillars gave it a more regal look. At over five thousand square feet, the house's size was only eclipsed by the vast two hundred and ninety acres surrounding it. I remember it being very scenic with a stone house at the front of the property that we used for storage, an open bay six-car garage just off of the winding driveway, a barn in the back of the property, along with a functioning garden and natural spring off to the side of our house. My father rented out most of the property surrounding our living area to local farmers to let their cattle graze. Nestled in this open land was an apple orchard. It was only a few acres in size, but helped to offset the rolling green hills and fields and gave it a very aesthetic appeal. It was not only a picturesque setting; it was also a very peaceful time in my life.

I have fond memories of hunting on our property with my dad, as well as camping and riding four-wheelers with my friends. My father was the ultimate provider, always working hard, making sure that I, or any member of my family, never wanted for anything. Looking back, I now realize that is how he showed his love for us. He never opened up emotionally to me. That just wasn't in his nature. He was a proud Jewish man, although non-practicing when it came to the religious aspects of his culture.

By the time I was in elementary school, I had taken a page from his book and stopped opening up emotionally as well. I guess it's true that the apple seldom falls far from the tree. Although, I'll never forget the one conversation we had where the walls came down a bit. I'm not sure who was more uncomfortable…him or me. We had a pet German Shepherd named Fang, who was a wonderful addition to the family, but sadly ended up with hip dysplasia and had to be put down.

When my father told me what had happened, he was short and to the point and delivered the news in a monotone, matter-of-fact manner. But I also remember vividly that he brought a candy bar to give to me during this talk to help ease the blow. I have no doubt to this day that my father loved me unconditionally. He just showed it in his own way.

My mother was the caregiver, around all of the time to take care of the family. I remember elaborate parties that she would throw at our house for all of our friends and my father's business associates. Most of the time, this entailed her hiring the most expensive caterers and servers to make sure the evening was flawless. I remember the adults always seemed like they enjoyed themselves at our parties. For me, they were just okay. As a kid, I would have much rather been playing outside than dressed up and on my best behavior in front of guests.

I had a provider and a caregiver for parents. With that combination, I never had to worry about anything. All my needs were always met. But sometimes my parents took things to extremes. I remember every fall, most parents would take their kids out shopping for new clothes for the upcoming school year. My parents were no exception. However, no stores in Winchester were good enough for us. We would hop in the car and drive to Northern Virginia, where there was a wider variety of retailers from which to choose. Macy's was always one of our first stops.

And Christmas was a whole other story. Even though neither one of my parents practiced any form of organized religion, (although technically, my mother was Catholic), Christmas was a big deal around our house. My parents would actually hire someone to play Santa Claus and arrive at our house in an actual sleigh on Christmas Eve. He would come inside and deliver presents to us (a few that we could open up that night), and then leave the rest for the next morning.

In the front of our house, we had a parlor off to the side that we would only use for entertaining purposes. Besides parties or holidays, the room remained vacant. It was a massive space with a twelve-foot ceiling that gave it the impression of being even larger than it already was. At Christmas, there would be a fully-decorated Douglas Fir in the far corner of the room with gifts surrounding it. And when I say surrounding it, I mean filling up about half of the room. On Christmas morning, my sister and I would actually get tired of unwrapping presents. That's how many there were.

But it wasn't just materialistic objects that were at my disposal. I also was allowed to do more than a lot of my friends were. As a grade-schooler, I remember going on my first date. Yes, you read that correctly. I went on my first date while my age was still in single digits. The love of my life back then was a girl named Jaelyn. I still remember our first date, staring across the booth at a local diner into her gorgeous blue eyes while we both drank our sodas. Granted her parents were sitting in the next booth, but I pretended we were all by ourselves. We also had a few dates where we would be driven to a vintage drive-in movie theater just outside of Winchester. Don't bother asking me what movies we saw. Jaelyn and I were too busy running around on the playground to watch the actual movie. But in my defense, they did have a sliding board in the shape of an elephant's trunk.

My childhood was a good time. I enjoyed living a privileged life. But even at this early age, my friends in school were starting to take notice. Whether it was my stylish clothes (as stylish as a grade-schooler can dress), or that I had every toy available or that my parents would sometimes pick me up from school in their Porsche or a combination of all three variables, bullying eventually started. I transitioned from being the cool rich kid to the spoiled, over-privileged doctor's son. Nobody likes to be bullied. And looking back, how I handled the situation may be what started me down a dark path.

Chapter 3

I'd like to say that along with the graduation to Robert
E. Aylor Middle School came maturity. But it didn't. And I'm
not pointing fingers at the maturity level of the students who
continued to bully me because of my 'privileged' status. I'm
pointing the finger directly at myself. I could have chosen to
take the high road when the teasing occurred. I could have
laughed it off and made fun of myself a time or two, hoping
that would be the end of it. But that's not what happened.

I bottled up the frustration and anger I felt every time
someone picked on me until I couldn't stand it anymore.
That's when the fighting started. It's not like I wanted to
fight, but it was the best solution I could come up with at the
time. Nobody was giving me any respect, so I was going to
have to earn it the old-fashioned way. I know now that this
isn't the way respect is earned, but 12-year-old me wasn't as
bright.

It wasn't just one fight that we're talking about here.
There were multiple episodes when I felt I had to prove my
manhood. It's awful, but I don't even remember the first

---

fight. They all kind of run together in my memories these days. There are only a few that stick out in my mind. Most of the fights back then happened in the halls between classes or on the playground…whenever you weren't under the immediate watchful eye of a teacher. One fight I remember is the exception to the rule. It was right in the middle of class when another student made a 'spoiled rich kid' comment to me.

Without hesitation, I stood up. My antagonist followed suit and within seconds, we were both swinging fists at each other. Before the teacher could intervene, we stumbled to the back of the room, arms intertwined with each other. We were both jockeying for position. Finally, I got it. I took his head and slammed it as hard as I could into a grey metal filing cabinet in the back of the room. It looked just like a professional wrestler slamming his opponent's head into the turnbuckle in the ring. The next thing I knew, blood was streaming profusely down his face. His head had been split wide open, and the fight was over.

This altercation led to the first of what would be a long list of school suspensions for me. This also led to my parents being worried about my actions, the friends I was running around with and my overall well-being. They tried to involve me in as many extracurricular activities as they could. I remember basketball camps, baseball camps and soccer camps. But none of them took. I would always have the top-of-the-line sports gear for each camp. The most expensive Louisville Slugger bat and Wilson glove for baseball. The most sought-after high-top sneakers that were en vogue at the time for basketball. And the best shin guards and jersey that money could buy for soccer. It's too bad I didn't use any of them. These sports just weren't for me.

I guess it's true that desperate times call for desperate measures, because my parents ended up sending me to a counselor. This didn't take either. In fact, I bottled up my feelings even more. If I wasn't going to talk to my family about my emotions, why would I open up to a complete stranger? It would be an understatement to say that all of my parents' interventions failed. I rejected anything they threw at me, and through it all, my behavior didn't change. There were still altercations (the politically-correct term for fights) in school. And I was starting to become somewhat of a bully myself. I hate to admit that now, but sometimes I felt I had to start a fight to avoid being picked on to begin with.

As my behavior began to grow more and more out of control, my parents felt they were out of answers. Nothing they tried had worked. They felt it was time for some tough love. A week before Christmas, my parents brought me to the Hurst House Adolescent Treatment Center. It was a subsidiary of our local hospital that helped young men and women. The licensed professionals that worked here would study, diagnose and work with anyone who was checked in. I say 'checked in' because I seriously doubt anyone would come here voluntarily.

What my parents didn't realize until after meeting with the doctors was that once someone was admitted, he or she was not allowed to leave the premises until a full-blown study and diagnosis was complete. After a battery of tests and analyses, I was diagnosed with bipolar disorder (a diagnosis that would later be deemed inaccurate, but that didn't matter at the time). My diagnosis and treatment took every bit of three weeks. Three weeks! For those of you doing the math…yes…this meant that I spent Christmas as a 12-year-old, not at home with friends and family, but under the watchful eyes of the staff at the Hurst House. It's hard to be away from family during the holidays as an adult, but as a 12-year-old…well, I wouldn't wish that on anybody.

In addition to the fact that I wouldn't be home for

Christmas, the experience itself was miserable for me. For starters, I had to forfeit the clothes I came in with for scrubs. That's right…medical scrubs. I was eventually able to earn my clothes back piece by piece via a point system based on good behavior. And for someone who was not used to too much structure in life, this was not the place to be. Every minute of every day was accounted for in some fashion. It was either in private counseling, group therapy, arts and crafts time or exercising. My parents were permitted visitations on a regular basis. They came to see me as often as they were allowed.

I distinctly remember them bringing one of my Christmas presents to me. It was the "Rump Shaker" CD by Wreckx-n-Effect. (Good luck not having that song stuck in your head for a while now.) I think I remember this so vividly because it was a gift from the outside world that I was so desperately missing at the time. My parents would also often bring me baseball cards when they visited. These helped me keep my homesickness at bay as much as possible.

Eventually, I was able to earn home visits. I did this by being a model patient at the Hurst House. Despite all the anger and resentment I had for being an involuntary guest, I fell in line. I engaged in the counseling. I contributed in group therapy. I gave them the person I thought they wanted to see. I did all of this, not because I thought I was helping myself. I did all of this because it was a means to an end. It was going to get me back home where I belonged. The Hurst House is a great place and has a track record of proven results for kids that belong there. But, in my opinion, I did not. If I learned anything from the Hurst House, it was how to manipulate a system for personal gain…a lesson that would come into play time and again in my life.

I was finally released from the Hurst House with the stipulation that I would come back for regular outpatient therapy…a concession I was more than willing to make. I was back at school not too much longer after Christmas break had ended and wound up with a new clique of friends to hang out with. They were different from me in the respect that they came from broken homes and lower income families. Most of them had pretty sad, hard-luck backstories. I guess the common denominator that brought us all together (besides the fact that none of us minded getting into a little bit of trouble now and then), was that we were struggling for some sort of identity, but didn't know exactly what we wanted.

I had morphed into my 'skater' phase at this point in my life. (Trust me. This is not the most embarrassing phase I would go through.) I wore baggy pants with oversized shirts. I had my head shaved tight all around, except for some black bangs I left hanging over my forehead. And yes, I'm cringing just remembering this look. The ironic thing is, I never remember actually having a skateboard. Oh well, at least I looked the part. After a few months, life was starting to get back on track for me. I had somewhat of a reputation. I was still being picked on, but not as much. I had a new group of friends. Little did I know that the carpet was about to be yanked out from underneath my feet.

Chapter 4

My parents called me into the kitchen and asked me to have a seat. I joined them at the table where they were both already sitting. My dad looked stoic as usual, but my mom looked pensive, like she was sad we had to be having this impromptu family meeting. Straight forward and to the point as always, my dad told me that I would not be returning to Robert E. Aylor Middle School after my sixth-grade year. I would be going to Randolph Macon Military Academy.

I was crushed. All the hard work and time I had invested to establish myself in middle school was about to be for nothing. But my parents felt they were out of alternatives, and this was the right decision. Randolph Macon was located in Front Royal, VA, about forty-five minutes from my house. Thankfully, my parents didn't make me live on campus. They drove me to and from school every day. Maybe they viewed this commute as quality family time that may have been missing for the past few months.

I spent my entire seventh-grade year at Randolph Macon and for the most part, it was non-eventful. Like any school, it had its pros and cons. For a guy searching for an identity, I definitely found one here...in appearance, at least. Adhering to the academy's strict dress code, I showed up to class each morning looking exactly like every other student. We all donned a blue blazer, button-down white collared shirt and khaki pants. Believe it or not, I actually earned good grades that year. Nothing crazy like the 'all-A' honor roll, but mostly all A's and B's. On the surface everything looked fine, but I just couldn't handle the formality of it all. Deep down, for whatever reason, I sincerely rejected the rigid structure being thrust upon my life. It sometimes reminded me of the Hurst House with all of its rules and accountability. So, just like my plan there, I decided to give everyone what they wanted, again only as a means to an end.

After a year of good grades, no behavioral issues and a new (not close...just new) set of friends I had met at the academy, I felt it was time to revisit the whole Randolph Macon decision with my parents. I was able to convince them, I'm sure with a little begging...no, scratch that...a lot of begging, that I was a changed man. I had learned my lesson and was ready to be assimilated back into the public school system. I wanted to return to Robert E. Aylor Middle School for my eighth-grade year.

After a long deliberation, my parents agreed to give me the opportunity to prove myself. I seemed like I had my head on straight. It was now time to prove it. I was heading back to my old school. Surely things would be much better this time around. And if you believe that, I have some oceanfront property in Kansas that I can get you a really good deal on.

By the time I returned from Randolph Macon, I had more than outgrown my 'skater' image that I had before I left. It was time for a new look. Don't ask me what my rationale was at the time, but I chose 'redneck.' And I spared no expense pulling off the look. I wore flannel shirts with tight

20

blue jeans. This is before skinny jeans were a thing, but I guarantee the ones I wore would come pretty close to being in that category. And, of course, the jeans were complimented with a variety of oversized brass belt buckles. Throw in genuine snakeskin boots, an oversized Stetson hat and a Chuck Norris-like trench coat, and you have a pretty good picture of how I looked that year.

This new country look brought a new set of country friends into my life. They enjoyed hunting and fishing, so it made perfect sense for me to invite these folks back to my house where we could engage in these types of activities on my parents' land. We hunted and fished a lot. Eventually, the hunting and fishing led to parties at my house. I say 'my house' but what I really mean is at the garage or some other place on the property where my parents weren't around. This is the first time I drank beer. My dad would have Coors Lights in the cooler in the garage and I would help myself to them. Other kids would sneak in their own beer and share so that my dad didn't notice too many beers missing.

My best friend out of this new group was a kid named Brad. We hit it off immediately and spent a lot of time together. Besides hanging out in groups at parties I'd host, we also spent a lot of time just him and me. We would ride four-wheelers, hunt, go fly-fishing and also drink beer together. Like any 14 year-old boy, we did a lot of stupid things together too. I know, you can argue that drinking beer at this age is stupid, but I can top that.

Brad and I got the bright idea one day that we were going to huff paint. It was supposed to be a quicker and better buzz than from drinking beer. And to be honest, unlike beer, we could buy everything we needed for this. All it took was a can of spray paint (or anything else that warns "Must be used in a well-ventilated area") and a plastic baggie. We sprayed some in the plastic bag and then held it over our mouths and noses and breathed it in until it did the job. This was the first real experience with anything stronger than alcohol. But as they say, there's a slippery slope when it comes to drugs, and unfortunately, this was just the beginning.

Brad and I continued engaging in activities like this and have the consequences to show for it. Once, we were camping on our property and got the bright idea to go four-wheeling in the middle of the night. We left our tent, our bonfire and our boom box, which was cranking some Hank Williams Jr., and took off into the night. We rode for about two hours before calling it quits and returning to our campsite. Only by the time we returned, our campsite wasn't there anymore. There wasn't much of anything there anymore.

Wind gusts had blown the flames from our bonfire on to some nearby hay bails that farmers used to feed their cattle. These hay bails acted as kindling and helped start a massive fire that burned twenty acres of land. Our tent, boom box and all of our belongings were completely destroyed. I remember the only thing standing in the middle of the torched twenty acres was a lone patch of trees, right in the middle. I then had the unenviable task of sneaking into my parents' bedroom, waking up my dad and letting him know that we now had twenty less acres of land to maintain.

Another time, Brad came over to my house and didn't leave for days. We didn't tell anyone either. Why did we do this? Who knows? It was just another stupid decision. It was probably so that we could hang out and huff paint or because we had already hung out and huffed paint, and it sounded like a reasonable plan. I had a Captain's bed in my room, and Brad would sleep in the underneath storage space at night. For the few nights he was there, I would sneak him food from the kitchen. Eventually, his parents, who were worried sick, touched base with my parents to find out if they had seen

Brad. After being confronted by my parents, I confessed, and Brad headed home…to what punishment, I can only imagine. Mine was bad enough, and my parents *knew* where I was.

That's what drugs do. They cause you to make stupid decisions. For most people, leaving a raging bonfire unattended in the middle of the night and burning down twenty acres of land would be one of the stupidest decisions they could make…but not me. For me, that decision was just the tip of the 'stupid' iceberg.

Chapter 5

My middle school years finally came to an end, and, like always, I celebrated in style. On the last day of school, my parents rented a stretch limo for me and a few of my closest friends. We left Robert E. Aylor and rode for hours. In eighth grade, you really don't have too many places to go on your own, so we just enjoyed being chauffeured around town with a quick stop at the arcade. Once I had a chance to show off my sweet Skeeball skills, we were right back to chilling in the limo again. Now that this chapter of my life was finished, I was more than ready to move on. The whirlwind was finally over. After two schools in three years with a brief layover at the Hurst House...I was definitely ready for some more stability from my high school years. I'm sure my parents agreed.

That summer was fairly uneventful. I became friends with a guy named Mitch who was a few years older than I was and drove a truck. We decided to go into business together for a few months and sell firewood. He had the transportation, and I had the resources (as long as I didn't burn down any more trees). We would cut firewood on my parents' property and then haul it off for sale in his truck. It was a nice way to make a little extra 'walking around' money, not that I ever needed any. But I enjoyed the work, and I enjoyed spending time with Mitch.

Of course, summer time means parties too. And I threw my fair share. Friends would come, and we'd spend evenings in my parents' garage or deeper into the woods with a bonfire (well-supervised). We would drink beer and occasionally liquor. And a few of us continued to huff paint too. Whatever the easiest high was, we'd chase. We were young and without a care in the world. Life was good, and we believed it would only get better.

Summer finally came to an end, and it was time to embark on the next leg of life's journey…high school. I couldn't wait. I would be able to start fresh. Find my real identity. Finally fit in. Well…you know what they say about the best-laid plans. The whole 'privileged' status that I was trying to shed became more apparent than ever. Status is a big deal to teenagers and it was obvious that anything I wanted, I was given the money to buy. This led to even more confrontations than I had in middle school. And my opponents seemed to get bigger and tougher too. I had a few scuffles here and there throughout my freshman year, but nothing major. For the most part, I kept my nose clean and really didn't give my parents a whole lot to worry about. Then my sophomore year rolled around.

I remember one fight (and I use the term loosely on this occasion), that happened that year. A student was giving me a hard time for being a 'spoiled rich kid' and I jawed back with him until it was obvious that some sort of action had to take place. They say, with age comes wisdom, and now that we were sophomores, we were old enough to realize that fights didn't have to happen on school property any more. That would make it too easy to get caught and punished.

Now, fights took place after school and anywhere besides school property. Most tenth graders had cars by this point, so it was easier to make this transition. My parents had given me an '87 GMC Sierra pickup truck they had bought for farm use on our property, but never used. It was in pristine condition when they handed me the keys. But that didn't stop me from adding a six-inch lift kit, thirty-five inch tires and a competition-worthy aftermarket stereo system, which for this special occasion was blaring, "Pump Up The Jam."

I drove my truck a mile down the road after school to meet my nemesis in an abandoned Jamesway store parking lot. High school students love a good fight, so it was no surprise that we drew a pretty big crowd that day. And the other students knew exactly what to do too. They all pulled their vehicles into the parking lot to form a loose circle with the front of the cars facing the middle. They then turned on all of their headlights for dramatic effect. It was show time. It was an overcast day, so the headlights really made the homemade arena stand out against the ominous grey skies.

My opponent and I circled each other for a moment or two while all the spectators yelled in the background. I honestly couldn't tell you if they were cheering for me or the other guy. Truth be told, I tuned them out. I was only focused on one thing… giving this fool the beat down he had coming. Both fists up, I ducked and weaved gracefully as I approached him in the center of the car circle. Before I even had time to react, he had caught me with a jab and a right cross, both connecting solidly on my face. I remember feeling an excruciating pain as the side of my head caught the rail of my truck on the way to the ground. And that is the last thing I remember about the fight.

I woke up later alone. All the cars were gone. The show was over. And I was lying in the middle of the parking lot, covered in blood. It was pouring down rain at this point and the raindrops mixed in with my bloody face to make me look a lot worse off than I actually was. Looking in the mirror, I definitely resembled a victim in some horror movie. I looked at my watch and realized that I had been out for about five minutes, and I was late picking up my sister from her school. I jumped in my truck and flew over to get her. Luckily, she was in middle school by this point, so she was old enough to come out to the parking lot when she saw my truck pull in. I sincerely doubt any teacher would have released her into my custody had I gone into the school to check her out. Getting yelled at by my little sister on the way home for being late seemed like the appropriate cherry on top of the fantastic day I had just finished.

This fight may seem like a random story to share, and believe me, I'd be much happier just including the fights that I won, but this one was significant because it changed me. I hated the fact that I lost. It wasn't just losing…it was losing so lopsidedly. And I never wanted to experience that feeling again. It wasn't the pain that bothered me. Let's be honest. I blacked out before the more severe pain had a chance to set in. It was the humiliation that bothered me. I was embarrassed in front of my peers, and my pride would not allow me to stand for that ever happening again. Going forward, I made a decision to never be embarrassed like that. And Heaven help the next person unlucky enough to cross my path. I know what you're thinking. Tough words for a guy who just got his butt handed to him. And I agree. But in any case, that was my mindset at the time. And it would get me into a lot more trouble.

Chapter 6

If I had to choose a time in my life that my drug use transitioned from recreational to dependent, it would probably have to be my sophomore year. I was still drinking and huffing paint occasionally. But this was the first time that I tried pot too. I had a group of friends I was hanging out with all the time at this point… a couple guys named Doug, Mark and John and a girl named Anna. They were the ones that introduced me to this drug, and we started to smoke it on a regular basis. We would get high on my parents' property once in a while, but mostly we would do it at one of their houses after school.

Smoking pot became such a habit with this crowd that I don't even remember hanging out with them much when we weren't getting high together. After a while, I really couldn't even tell you if I enjoyed their company or not. They seemed cool, but we were always in an altered state of mind. Who knows if we really even had anything in common or not. This became painfully obvious one evening when the gang was over at my place getting high. We started to smoke some pot in the garage, but ran out early. I vividly remember looking around at these folks and wondering, *"Do I even like you, or am I just hanging out with you because you can score some weed for us?"*

I recall being so bored with my company at that moment that I had to do something about my sober state. I decided to sneak into my house and steal some pills from my mom's medicine cabinet. I found a bottle of Lorcet Plus, which she had a prescription for. Lorcet Plus is a combination of hydrocodone and acetaminophen. Hydrocodone is a pain medication and acetaminophen is a less potent pain reliever that increases the effects of hydrocodone. The combination of these drugs is a medicine used to relieve moderate to severe pain.

The warning label on the bottle is nothing short of a small novel, listing all the dangers and side effects of this medication. One pill typically gets the job done and relieves pain. But we wanted more. So just to be sure we were getting the most bang for our buck, we each popped five of these bad boys and waited to see just how good we would feel. To say the results were mixed would be an understatement. I watched the rest of my group get violently ill from these pills. There were a few moments when I wasn't sure if I was going to need to call 9-1-1 or not. But the Lorcet Plus had the opposite effect on me. Once the narcotic took, I experienced the absolute best high I had ever known. It was a euphoric feeling, and all I knew was that I wanted a lot more of it. But I couldn't just deplete my mom's stash, so I started planning on just how to make that happen.

In the meantime, school was school. I was earning decent grades, and I hadn't been in any more fights since the Jamesway fiasco. Maybe after that display, folks just figured, *"What's the point? This guy couldn't fight his way out of a wet paper bag."* If that *is* what happened, then everyone got the memo except for one particular student in my Vocational

Agriculture class, or VO-AG for short. Embarrassingly enough, I originally signed up for this class hoping to learn enough horticultural tips to be able to grow my own marijuana plants. That's how much pot was consuming my time. It turned out that I really enjoyed this class except for the aforementioned student who shared it with me. We had been running our mouths toward each other for weeks until the point of culmination was inevitable.

VO-AG didn't take place in a regular classroom most of the time. We were usually in the workshop area. It was a massive open-spaced room with giant bay windows, raised ceilings, concrete floors and industrial-strength ventilation systems. We were in the workshop on the day of our encounter. My antagonist walked past me, made a crude comment and continued on his way. I remembered the embarrassment I had felt from my last fight and knew I was not going to allow that to happen again. I felt a rage consume me that I had never known before, and I zoned out. I don't remember picking up a 2x4 block of wood off of one of the table saws. I don't remember swinging it as hard as I could at his head. And I don't remember doing it multiple times.

But I'm told by several witnesses that is what happened. When I snapped out of my blind rage, our teacher was hunched over the other student, trying to help him stop the bleeding. His head was split wide open from his hairline to halfway down the left side of his face. Other students were frantically trying to sop up as much blood as they could with the generic brown paper towels from the dispenser on the wall. There was so much blood everywhere that it looked like they were just smearing it around instead of actually wiping it up. The scene continued to look more and more horrific. I remember looking at the student I had just attacked and feeling remorse. I wanted to teach him a lesson, but nothing like this. I didn't remember any of this, but regretted it, nonetheless.

I was sent to the principal's office, but that was the least of my problems. This wasn't just a school issue. This was assault. That made it a police matter. Law enforcement was called in, along with my victim's parents and mine. My dad was able to talk the other student's parents out of pressing charges by agreeing to perform free cosmetic surgery to cover up the scar that was going to be left by the damage I had inflicted. After the surgery, the other student was okay, although we never spoke again. I was, however, kicked out of VO-AG and suspended from school for a while.

After that incident, nobody in school ever challenged me to a fight. I hated what I had done, but it was nice after all these years not to be bothered with fighting anymore. Besides, without distractions like these, I could finally move ahead with what I had been planning. I wanted to meet my friends' dealer. The one who always sold them the pot that we would smoke together. I wanted to meet him for two reasons. Reason #1: I was still chasing the high of the Lorcet Plus and wanted to know what other drugs were out there that I hadn't tried yet. And I was up for trying anything. Cocaine, crystal meth, LSD…it didn't matter. I'd give it a shot. Reason #2: I know this sounds crazy, but at that time, the life of a dealer sounded glamorous to me. The perceived power, money, prestige, respect…I wanted a taste of that. I knew that all I needed was a face-to-face meeting with this dealer and it would be the beginning of a beautiful relationship.

I have never been more wrong in my entire life.

Chapter 7

As the drug use between my friends and me became more habitual than recreational, I knew it was time for a change. Opportunity was right in front of me. I just had to reach out and grab it. And I'm not talking about the opportunity for an education. The fact of the matter was that school was becoming an afterthought for me. I felt more and more disengaged each day. I had no intention of earning my high school diploma just so I could go work a 40-hour per week job living paycheck to paycheck. I had much more ambitious goals.

I knew what my friends and I were spending each week for drugs, and I realized that our dealer, or any decent dealer for that matter, had to be making money faster than he could spend it. That was the life I was looking for. At this point, I had never even met our contact. All I knew was that his name was Joey and that he lived in Northern Virginia about an hour outside of Winchester. I had asked several times for a meeting with him, but was told he was extremely cautious about meeting new people. So I was forced to play the waiting game for a while. This anticipation only fueled my fire of wanting to be on Joey's side of the fence. He was obviously a shot caller and a decision maker. Looking back, I don't think I wanted to meet Joey as much as I wanted to *be* Joey.

So while I was forced to wait for a face-to-face meeting, I decided it was time to start preparing for my new role. This began with getting rid of my GMC pickup truck and upgrading to a Z 28 Camaro. And it was sweet. Green with a tan leather interior and of course, another aftermarket, competition-worthy stereo system. This was a slick ride. Don't get me wrong...the pickup was a jewel too. But this new vehicle more accurately reflected the image I was going for. And I must have been doing something right, because it wasn't long after that I got word that Joey was willing to meet with me. This was it...my first glimpse behind the curtain. I had butterflies in my stomach, but I wasn't going to let nerves get the best of me. I was going to make the most out of this encounter and win Joey's trust.

I drove to Northern Virginia with Anna. On the way, I spent the whole time going over in my head what I was going to say, how I would answer any questions he had and what I hoped to take away from the meeting. It was honestly like going to a job interview and hoping that you don't completely blow it. We arrived at Joey's townhouse, which was located in a middle to lower-end neighborhood. His wife, April, greeted us at the door. I don't know why this surprised me, but it did. I had placed Joey up on some grand pedestal. To find out that he was married (and actually had children too), somehow humanized him a little in my eyes. But don't get me wrong...I was still in awe of the man. I knew he was my ticket to the next level.

Introductions were made, and a few simple pleasantries were exchanged. Then, after minutes of arriving, Joey invited me to join him upstairs while the girls waited where they were. This made my heart start racing. Yes, I desperately wanted to meet this guy and make a good impression, but in reality I had no idea who this guy was or what he was about. Blindly following him into another room in a house I'd never been to before in a city an hour away from home…something didn't feel right. Was this a setup? Could Joey actually be an undercover cop? Or worse…were some of his friends waiting upstairs to mug me? Believe me, these were just two of about a hundred scenarios that crossed my mind as I cautiously walked behind him up the stairs. He led me down a hallway and into what appeared to be the master bedroom. My nerves became even shakier as he shut and locked the door behind us.

Joey asked me if I was a cop, and I told him that I wasn't. That seemed good enough for him. He pulled out a mini zip lock baggie filled with white powder from his dresser and held it up at eye level for me to see as if he were showing it off. "You do coke?" Joey asked. "Sure," I said, trying to sound casual. The truth is that I hadn't tried cocaine at all in my life up to this point, but was scared that an answer like that would make me look like a rookie and that wasn't the impression I was going for. "Good," Joey said. He then laid down a mirror, poured the cocaine on to it and started dividing the powder up into lines with a razor blade.

Joey handed me a rolled-up one hundred-dollar bill. I realized this was a strategic maneuver on his part. If I had been lying about being a cop, this would certainly weed me out. This power play made me like and respect Joey even more. And I hadn't even gotten to know him yet. I took the rolled up bill, bent down toward the line closest to me and snorted it completely. Joey was smiling as if I'd passed some test, then took the bill from me and followed suit. Then it was time to discuss business.

I told him that I would like to start buying stronger

product from him than just pot. I wanted whatever he had, and I was willing to buy in bulk. I wanted to do exactly what Joey was doing, but didn't think this was stepping on his toes. After all, he was still going to be getting paid...even more. He seemed lukewarm to the idea at first. Then after some more discussion, he began to appear aloof to the entire proposal. Maybe he had enough customers. Maybe doing this kind of business with someone he just met was considered premature. Maybe he just didn't like me. Whatever the reason, I could tell I was losing him. That's when I decided to play my trump card.

"Have you ever thought about getting into pills?" I asked. This seemed to grab his attention. "Sure," he said. "And I guess you'd want to buy those from me too, right?" "No," I replied. "I want to be the guy to supply you with them." It was a bold response and somewhat cocky, but it did its job. Joey stared at me as if he were studying me to see if I was legitimate or just wasting more of his time. This was my moment. I was going all in here. My gaze was locked on his and neither one of us was breaking eye contact. After what literally felt like minutes of staring, Joey smiled. "And how would you do that?" he asked. And just like that, I knew I was in. I explained to him that my father was a physician, and that I had access to his prescription pads. I could provide forged prescriptions for anything we wanted if he, in return, could find a few less-than-ethical pharmacies who wouldn't scrutinize our requests too much.

"I think I may know a few places that would be willing to accommodate us," he said. He stuck out his hand to shake. This was it. I had done it. I was part of the inner circle now. But I wasn't finished. There was still some more business to be discussed. "Now we just have to talk pricing," I said. I was happy I had gotten this far, but wanted to make sure I wasn't going to be taken advantage of either. Just as I was feeling good about the arrangement, Joey threw me a curveball. "Whoa, whoa, whoa. Slow down there," he said with another smile. "Just because I've agreed to this, doesn't mean it's a done deal. I still have to run this past my boss. We'll have to wait and see what Big Mike says."

"Who's Big Mike?" I asked. "Big Mike's the head of the family," Joey replied. "He makes the decisions, and the rest of us carry them out."

"Well, when can I meet Big Mike?" I asked.

"You don't just meet Big Mike. You have to earn a meeting with him. I'll talk to him and see if he's interested in your arrangement and get back in touch with you. That's all I can do for now. I'll be in touch."

I bought an eight ball (3.5 grams) of cocaine from Joey to close out the meeting. We rejoined the girls downstairs for a few more pleasantries, and then Anna and I headed back home. I had a permanent smile on my face the entire trip. I had just gotten my foot into the door of a legitimate crime family. Life was good.

Chapter 8

Weeks passed, and I still hadn't received an invitation to meet with Big Mike. But that was okay. I knew it was going to happen, and in the meantime, I was determined to become a major earner for him. I started out buying an eight-ball of coke from Joey on a weekly basis, but that order soon turned into at least an ounce at a time. My customer base was continually growing. I would go to different parties around town and quickly figure out who was using and who wasn't. I would then make it a point to get to know the folks who were and let them know that I had a supply that could meet their demand, should they ever want to do business in the future.

It's funny. Today, I am actively involved in several business networking groups, and the business principles are basically the same. Meet new people, explain to them what services you provide, and let them know you'd be interested in doing business with them in the future. The only difference now is that what I do is legal, and it actually helps people instead of hurting them. But the principles remain the same nonetheless.

I was also being smart about it. I took a page out of Joey's book and had a few select "earners" of my own. They would always make the actual hand-off. I never got involved in passing drugs to anyone I didn't know. Most of our customers were older people we would meet at parties, primarily in the 20's, 30's and 40's. I was becoming the 'Joey' of Winchester. And it felt great. People started to realize that I was 'connected.' If you wanted something, I was the man to talk to. Maybe not directly if I didn't know you, but word was spreading that I had some stroke. I felt like Robert DeNiro's character in *GoodFellas*. (The cool young one in the beginning, not the creepy old one in the end).

With all the trips to Northern Virginia to pick up new orders and the countless parties, excuse me, networking opportunities, I found myself spending the night with friends most of the time. It got to the point where I was only heading home once a week or so. And that was usually to pick up a change of clothes or if I was really feeling ambitious, to do a load of laundry. Let's be honest, it was usually just to pick up a change of clothes. My parents didn't approve of me staying out for days at a time, but it also didn't come as a shock to them. They still tried to persuade me to stay home and to add some sense of normalcy to my life, but they had been fighting this rebellious streak in me for years now and were starting to realize there wasn't much more they could do.

Along with bigger orders from Joey came a larger profit margin for me. What I was making each week was enough to support my personal habit and then some. I was living the dream. More money than I had ever earned *and* free drugs. Life just kept getting better and better. And then, just like that, as if things couldn't improve…I received a call from Joey. I was climbing the corporate ladder and moving more and more product each week. And because of this, Big Mike had agreed to meet with me.

The meeting was scheduled for the next day at a location to be disclosed to me at the last minute for security purposes. Joey informed me to dress nice, wait for his call and to not be late. Failing to abide by any of these would be a sign of disrespect. I made sure I was going to be prepared. I went out and bought a brand new suit. There was no time to have it custom tailored, but I found one that was a close enough fit to make it look like it was. I even bought some new "bling" to complete the ensemble. Throw in an expensive oversized watch, a new gold chain large enough to make Mr. T jealous and a pinky ring, and I was good to go. Yes, I wore a pinky ring. I admit it. Now I would like to move on and never mention this again. Thank you.

I laid in bed all night, playing the scene out in my mind of how things would go down. I needed to show respect, but not fear. I had to show him that I had ambition but was still a team player. I wanted him to realize that I was smart, but not arrogant. After hours of anticipating the different ways this conversation would flow, I finally fell asleep. And then dreamt about it some more.

I headed out on U.S. Route 66 East on my way to meet Big Mike early the next day. It was two hours before Joey said he would be calling me, but I remembered what Joey told me about not being late. Surely, the earlier I was, the more respect it would show, right? Just then, my cell phone rang. It was Joey.

"Hey!" he said. "Have you left for the meeting yet?"

"Just getting ready to," I replied. I was a little embarrassed for him to find out that I had already left and just planned on driving around until I received his call.

"Good. I'm glad I caught you. I've got good news and bad news."

I've always hated when people start off with that phrase because almost every time the bad news trumps the good news. "What is it?" I asked.

"The bad news is that the meeting is off." My grip on the steering wheel tightened as I felt the frustration start to build up inside of me. Joey continued talking. "One of Big Mike's guys got a tip that the cops know about the meeting and are planning on being there. It's better for everyone that we just stay away today."

"Got it. What's the good news?"

"Big Mike gave us the green light on using your dad's prescription pads."

"That's great, but when do I get my sit-down with him?"

"Don't know. Big Mike's funny about these types of things. Honestly, I'm surprised he agreed to a meeting with you this early. But the best way to guarantee the reschedule is to impress him with our new venture."

"Got it," I said and hung up the phone.

I turned the car around and headed back home. It took a little while for the disappointment and anger to subside. But after they had, I realized the golden opportunity I now had. I was completely looking past the dangers or ramifications of stealing a doctor's prescription pads and forging his name. I was only seeing dollar signs and opportunity for advancement in my new career. To make this work, I was going to have to get all my ducks in a row and do this the right way. First step: Learn how to forge prescriptions.

I'd like to tell you that Big Mike and Joey sent me a

forging expert and we had some clandestine meeting in an empty parking garage at 2:00 AM where he passed on all of his wisdom to me. But it was nothing that dramatic. To find out everything I needed to know about how to successfully replicate a doctor's signature on script pads…I Googled it. There was nothing glamorous or sexy about it. I simply looked it up online. I remember clearing out my browser history when I was done just to cover my tracks. Like that would be what I had to worry about if I were to ever get caught.

Now I had the knowledge. I just needed the pads. This was as easy as a trip back home. My family was happy to have me back for an evening and to share a home-cooked meal with me. Little did they suspect that clean clothes weren't the only things I'd be taking with me when I left. I knew my dad kept some pads in his office, so I helped myself to one. Hey, I didn't want to be greedy…or draw attention to the fact that more than one of his pads may or may not be missing.

At this point, I knew what I was doing. I had the pads. I knew how to forge them to make them look authentic. I even knew what kind of pills I would be prescribing. All I needed now was a clear focus. And there was just one thing keeping me from that. It became crystal clear that in order to focus on the job at hand and to do it well…I had to drop out of high school.

Chapter 9

I sat in my car in the school parking lot and fired up a joint. Classes had already started, but I didn't care. What did it matter if I were tardy? I was getting ready to march in and officially quit. Did I mention that it was spring and that there were literally a few weeks left until graduation? And did I also mention that I had passing grades in all my classes? Which meant that all I had to do was show up and not do anything incredibly stupid, and I would graduate from high school. But as the pot smoke filled the car, the decision to drop out of school didn't feel as idiotic as it does in retrospect. At the time, it felt like the only logical choice.

What was I going to do with some worthless diploma? Use it to get a job? I already had one, and it paid a heck of a lot more than any other job I could get using my high school education. No thanks. My mind was made up. I headed into the school, walked right past the class I was supposed to be in at that moment and proceeded to the guidance department. I told the first guidance counselor I saw that I wanted to talk to someone about quitting. At first, the department thought it was a joke. Why would anyone in his right mind quit with just a few weeks left? Once they realized that I was deadly serious, they flew into intervention mode. I had to talk to several counselors and other faculty members. My parents were called and made aware of this occurrence as well.

After what felt like an eternity, the counselor I was dealing with threw in the towel. After all, I was eighteen at this point. There was legally nothing they could do to keep me enrolled. They gave me the proper paperwork to sign, and I gladly did so. I walked out of school that day an emancipated man. No longer would I be a slave to their rules and useless curriculum. I had my freedom, and it was time to start making my millions.

I stopped in to see my parents later that evening. To say they were disappointed with my decision would be an understatement. But again, I was eighteen, and there was nothing they could do to stop me. They reinforced everything the school counselors had told me earlier in the day about it being a decision I would regret the rest of my life…blah, blah, blah. I'd heard enough of this talk in one day to last a lifetime. The bottom line was that the decision was made, and it was time to get to work. I planned on breaking out the script pad the next day.

After a lot of practice, I really didn't have my dad's signature down to an art. But let's be honest, all doctor's signatures pretty much look alike. Just scribble a bunch of sloppy loops and then throw a dot or two on top for a possible "i" or "j" and you're fine. I signed my dad's name and wrote the order for thirty 40mg Oxycontin pills. Research had taught me that anything around thirty pills or less would not raise any red flags.

I drove to a local pharmacy the next day and with script in hand, entered the building. I wasn't nervous at all. The thought of being caught was completely shadowed by the sheer awesomeness of this plan. I walked up to the counter and handed the paper to the pharmacist, an older gentleman. He looked at the script and then back at me, as if he were studying a fake driver's license of someone trying to buy beer underage. I was unfazed. I believed in my plan. It was foolproof. He eventually took the script and asked me if I wanted to wait or come back for the pills. I told him I'd be back. An hour later I returned, picked up my pills and then sat in my car and smiled. This gig was even easier than I had imagined it to be.

These pills sold on average for a dollar per milligram. With what I had paid out of pocket for all thirty, I stood to make a substantial profit, even with Big Mike's and Joey's cut. Compound this with the number of times I planned to do it, and I would soon be financially set for life. And I didn't even need a high school diploma to figure out *this* math.

The following few weeks proved very profitable for me. I was filling prescriptions a few times a week, but never at the same pharmacy twice. I thought the cocaine market was fruitful, but it was nothing compared to how in demand pills were. I could barely keep them in stock. Business was booming. Supply was easy to come by, and demand stayed extremely high. I would see Joey on a weekly basis to give him his and Big Mike's cut and to buy more coke. Just because the pill market was my bread & butter now didn't mean I was going to abandon other revenue sources. I was a businessman now.

Okay…to say that I was a businessman at this point may be a little premature. A *true* businessman would probably know how much of a cut was being taken and how much he was making as a net profit. To be honest with you, I was so in awe of this new role that I would just hand over all the cash I had earned the previous week to Joey, and he would count it all out. Then he would pull out a certain amount and give back to me. Sometimes he would throw in a few extra hundred-dollar bills and call it my bonus for a job well done. But even with that, I could have still been getting ripped off for all I knew. I think Joey had mentioned a standard 50/50 split when we first started, but who knows? They could have been taking eighty percent for all I cared. I was in the game now, and that's all that mattered. And I also rationalized the fact that I really couldn't put a price tag on the guidance and protection I was receiving.

I knew it was just a matter of time before Joey and Big Mike recognized my value and would jump on board to open up even more doors in other territories. I hoped it would be soon because I knew Winchester was a small pond for a big fish like me. It was only a matter of time before I exhausted my resources and needed to find other pharmacies to fill my scripts. *Or* I could increase my prescriptions. I knew it could be risky, but a few strategic orders of sixty or ninety pills may not be too greedy. After all, no one had seemed to bat an eye at an order of thirty up to this point. How much worse would sixty be?

Another reason I wanted to up the ante at this point is that my personal usage had increased tremendously too. I would snort a pill now and then when I started, but now I was taking oxy every day. It was starting to take a toll on me mentally *and* physically. I was at the point where I wasn't taking oxy because I wanted to anymore. It was because I had to. It was what was keeping me balanced...or so I believed at the time. So to make sure I had enough pills was of paramount importance.

I kept my composure and wrote out a script for sixty Oxycontin pills. I dropped off the prescription at a new pharmacy and even kept my composure as I picked up my sixty pills an hour later. The pharmacist didn't so much as flinch at an order of sixty pills. So hey, if nobody cares that I doubled my order, why not just do it again? Nobody will care about a prescription for one hundred and twenty pills. Brilliant logic, I know.

I wrote the script out for one hundred and twenty Oxycontin pills and drove to the next pharmacy on my list. I walked in and dropped off the script. The young girl behind the counter asked me if I'd like to wait while they filled the prescription. I told her I'd just come back later. She then looked at the script and studied it for another moment. She shot me a weak smile and then disappeared to the back.

I walked out of the pharmacy with the sinking feeling in my gut that I had just been busted. I don't know why, but I knew that the pharmacist was calling my dad's office to verify the prescription. Or maybe it was just the Oxy making me paranoid. Maybe everything was fine after all. I sat in my car in the parking lot and pondered my next move. Should I come back to pick up the prescription or just cut my losses? I decided on the latter. I was going to get out of Dodge and plan my next move.

If the pharmacy had, in fact, called in my script, then not only did they know I was a fraud, but they also had my handsome mug on video from one of the several cameras located inside the store. It wouldn't take the police very long to figure out who I was. And it didn't. There was an APB out for me within the hour.

Chapter 10

I laid low for a few days after I found out that I was a wanted man. I wasn't sure what my long-term plan was, but my short-term one was to simply not get caught. I bounced around from friend's house to friend's house, lying low as much as I could. Once I felt the heat had died down a little, I paid a visit to my parents' house to pick up a few things. I went during the day when I knew they would both be at work, and the house would be empty. I figured this would be the safest time to get in and out without being noticed.

And I was right…kind of. I wasn't noticed entering the house. Leaving was another story. Waiting for me in the driveway as I walked out the front door was a sheriff. To this day, I don't know if he had been staking out the house or if they were just doing routine checks, but either way, this guy was at the right place at the right time, or I was just at the *wrong* place at the *wrong* time.

The crime that I was officially charged with was uttering a forged prescription and attempting to obtain drugs by fraud. And it was indeed a felony. They couldn't charge me for possession because I never went back to pick up the pills. That was about my only silver lining in this whole mess. Because this was my first offense, and I had a relatively-clean record up to this point, I was sentenced to thirty days incarceration. This was to be served at the local Frederick County Regional Jail. Thirty days. When I heard this it was like a punch to the gut. By Mike Tyson. With brass knuckles. Thirty days was an eternity. They might as well have sentenced me to thirty years.

If the movie *Escape From Alcatraz* had taught me anything, it was that jail was the last place I ever wanted to be. They were dark and dingy and looked like they hadn't been cleaned since 1972. Every inmate was huge and looking for a fight. The guards were on the take and always looked the other way when riots started, which seemed to happen on a pretty regular basis. And don't even get me started on the shower scenes.

The first myth was debunked as soon as I walked into the facility in my new green jumpsuit. The place was divided into pods, and the one that I was escorted to was…clean. In fact, it was so clean that the smell of disinfectant was in the air. This was a pleasant surprise, and I was hoping this meant that the movie scripts were so off-base that I had nothing to worry about. Maybe this would be a tolerable stay after all.

The next myth that was proved false was that all the inmates weren't in lockdown. All of the cell doors were open, but only a few inmates were actually in them. The cells surrounded a large open-spaced common area where it looked like everyone else, about one hundred altogether, were gathered. Some inmates were working out. Others were playing cards. Some were reading. And some were playing dominoes.

My guard led me to my cell, which just happened to be

one of the ones with an inmate still occupying it. The older black man lying on the bottom bunk just stared at me for a moment after the guard left us. I thought it was rude that the guard hadn't made formal introductions for us before he left, but then I remembered where I was. This place and the people in it probably weren't too concerned with niceties. I wasn't sure whether or not to stare back or to divert eye contact. Prison movies had sent mixed messages for this sort of etiquette. However, to my relief, my new roommate broke the silence.

"I'm Will," he said in a monotone voice. "You've got top bunk."

That was as warm and friendly as our first meeting was, and I was grateful that it was *that* cordial. I hopped up on the top bunk and checked out my new home. It was about six feet by eight feet with nothing but a bunk bed, a sink and a toilet. This arrangement would be cozy to say the least.

The next few days seemed to take forever. I mainly kept to myself and really hadn't talked to anyone besides Will. Depression had set in, and on top of that I was feeling nauseated most of the time. After the cold sweats started, I finally figured out what was happening. I was going through withdrawal. I was so used to having some sort of controlled substance in my system that after a few days of going cold turkey, I was definitely feeling the effects. To my surprise, withdrawal had also affected my social skills. I was so used to being in an altered state of mind for the good part of each day, that I had to relearn what it was like to interact with people socially. And remember, I wasn't in the most desirable social setting. The guys I met were serving time for anything from DUI to assault to possession to failing to pay child support. It was somewhat comforting to know that I wasn't locked up with the truly violent criminals like the murderers and such. But I also realized that our environment was not completely immune to violence either.

In the meantime, Will had become a decent friend to me. He seemed like a trustworthy guy and for whatever reason seemed to have taken a liking to me and took me under his wing. He laid down some of the rules so I wouldn't make any rookie mistakes. For instance, there was one question you never answered. *When are you getting out?* The reason for this was that the shorter time you're in for, the more folks would resent you. For instance, if someone finds out that you're getting out in two days, and they have two more years, they'd either write you off or do something to get you in trouble to extend your stay. Apparently misery *does* love company and even more so behind bars. I took Will's advice to heart. I didn't even tell *him* when I was getting out until the day I was released.

The days turned into weeks, and my time there was pretty uneventful. My friends came to visit me once, but my family visited as often as was allowed. I don't know if I relayed it to them effectively at the time or not, but these visits meant the world to me and helped me stay grounded during this time. Lockdown was at 10:00 PM each night, and our cell doors were locked until 6:00 AM the next day. I found myself spending a lot of my time playing cards. My social skills had come back to me to the point where I could fit in with most folks, and my nausea had subsided. I was in the home stretch now. I only had a week left on my sentence when my first 'incident' occurred.

I was in the middle of a game of spades with five other inmates when a buddy of mine gave me a good-natured shove. I say he was a buddy because he actually was. He and I got along pretty well, and the shove was just in good fun. So I did what any buddy would do and got up and shoved him back. I learned it was okay to have fun in jail, but you never made it look like you were a pushover. My shove led to another shove by him, which was answered by a retaliatory shove by me, and before I knew it we were locked up and jockeying for position on one another. I really don't think either one of us knew if we were still horsing around or if this was a real fight at this point. But neither of us was about to give an inch to the other.

Other inmates immediately took their positions at the wall's perimeter to watch for guards. They knew that if one of us got in trouble, everyone did. I finally mustered enough strength to pull my sparring partner down to the ground. The only problem was that he landed squarely on top of me. His elbow jammed hard into my side and fractured one of my ribs. However, as soon as that happened, our lookouts let us know that the guards were returning. I jumped back into my chair, despite the pain, and continued the card game. It looked like business as usual by the time the guards made their walk-through. Despite the pain in my side and my shortness of breath, I knew that I was going to have to suck it up and deal with the pain. If I asked for any medical attention, there would be an investigation into what happened, and as I stated before, it wouldn't just be me who got into trouble.

I sucked up the pain until my release date a few days later. I said my goodbyes to Will and thanked him for watching over me. My parents met me in the front of the police station and took me home. You would have thought that spending thirty days in the big house would have been a wake-up call, but all I cared about was getting back to business. I was hoping this mishap hadn't ruined my relationship with Joey, or even worse, Big Mike. But these issues could wait another day to be answered. It turned out that even though I hadn't heard from my friends nearly as much as I had my family, they had decided to throw me a 'coming home' party that night. Little did I know that this night would be far worse than my entire thirty-day stint in jail.

Chapter 11

It broke my mom's heart that after bringing me home from jail I would choose to go out and spend my first night of freedom with my friends rather than my family. Even though my friends had not come to see me nearly as much as my family during my incarceration, I still chose to be with them that evening…just one more poor decision to add to the list at that time in my life. I felt a little guilty about leaving the house that night, but my friends had taken the time to throw me a party. I had to show up. I was the guest of honor after all.

The party was at Anna's grandmother's house, where she was living those days. All my old buddies were there to greet me and welcome me home. They asked me a few questions about what it was like on the 'inside' but mostly we just hung out and talked and laughed. It was a relief to be with my friends again. They treated me like nothing had happened. It wasn't long before they brought out the party favors and offered me some coke. I had just gone thirty days without indulging in any drug, not by choice mind you, but without indulging nonetheless. I was ready for a good, long overdue high.

I followed a couple of my buddies to a bedroom and snorted my first line in a month. The rush came right back to me. In just thirty days, I had forgotten how much I enjoyed this feeling. I followed up my first line with a second to make up for lost time. I felt even better than I could imagine...for a while. After about twenty minutes or so, I started feeling anxious. I was sweating a little, and my heart started racing. I guess my body wasn't reacting well after being dry for a month. I decided I needed to do something to balance out the cocaine.

I hit up another friend of mine for some Valium and chased a few with a beer. This seemed to somewhat level me off. So what was the next logical step? More cocaine, of course. Now I know what you're thinking. If making poor decisions were an Olympic event, I would have more gold medals than Michael Phelps. But at the time, it made perfect sense. Heck, if anything, I was being responsible by managing my high.

I snorted another couple of lines, and lo and behold, the pattern continued. I started feeling shaky and somewhat paranoid and realized I had to come down a little. No problem. A few more Valiums and I was rock steady again. I had everything under control.

After another hour of partying, Joey showed up. I was overwhelmed with mixed emotions when I saw him. On one hand, I was flattered he had shown up to welcome me back. On the other hand, I didn't know how he was going to act toward me since getting pinched. As Joey grabbed a beer, I made my way across the room to him. He greeted me with a smile and brought my handshake in for a hug. We made small talk for a few minutes. It didn't take long for him to ask me what I had shared with my attorney and the police. He asked specifically if his or Big Mike's names had come up. I told him they hadn't, and that I took full responsibility for everything. And this was the truth. I hadn't sold out anyone. I did the crime, and I did the time. I know that's a cheesy cliché, but in this case it was the truth. Joey asked me a few questions about my time in lockup, and that was it. He told me he'd be in touch soon and left to talk with some other folks at the party. I felt like he was being a little standoffish with me, but maybe that was just the coke making me paranoid. Either way, it was good to see Joey and know that I had not completely burned that bridge.

I rejoined the rest of my friends at the party, and the cycle of cocaine and Valium continued throughout the rest of the evening. Up and down. Up and down. I had really gotten the hang of this. Even after thirty days of being clean. It was just like riding a bike. It all came back to me. I knew my tolerance, and I knew what I could handle. And in my mind I was handling it like a champ. That's the last thing I remember before waking up in the hospital.

I was disoriented when I woke up, and it took me a moment to realize where I was. My parents were sitting by my bed. Their eyes were red and swollen from crying. I instinctively asked them what I was doing here, and my mom's voice cracked as she told me that I had overdosed. It turns out that the doctors had to pump my stomach to remove all the drugs from my system. My parents started to cry again. I think it was a combination of the pain of seeing their son almost die and the relief to see me wake up.

My disorientation soon turned to anger. I was beyond furious that I was in the hospital, and that this had happened to me. I knew that I only had myself to blame, but this only fueled my rage. Then my thoughts turned to Joey. Had he been at the party when I overdosed? Does he know I'm in the hospital? Is he disappointed in me? For some reason, at that moment, Joey's approval was more important to me than anything. I really hoped I had not let him down.

I demanded to be discharged from the hospital. Against my parents' and the doctors' wishes, I signed the required paperwork, got dressed and left. I called one of my friends to come pick me up and give me a ride back to the party. He filled me in on what had happened on the drive back. I was told that I had passed out and nobody could revive me. They tried for an hour, but didn't have any luck. Then, in their infinite wisdom, they picked me up and dumped my limp body into the street just down from the house where we were partying. I guess they thought that if my body wasn't found in the house, they all had plausible deniability of the situation.

At least they didn't leave me there to die. They put a quick, anonymous call into my parents and told them where I was and that I needed to be brought to the emergency room immediately. And like any good parents would do, mine jumped in the car and sped to where I was. They managed to drag me into the backseat and drove me to the hospital where the doctors immediately pumped my stomach and hooked me up with several IVs to try and help me regain consciousness.

When I arrived back at the party, I received a hero's welcome. It was perhaps a more heartfelt 'welcome home' than when I had arrived earlier in the night. Everyone gave me hugs and told me how happy they were that I was alright. I think that everyone was genuinely glad to see me, but I couldn't help but notice that the party had continued in my absence. I could have died, but the party never stopped. That thought didn't stay in my head for long. I was just happy to be out of the hospital and back at the party.

I was eighteen years old and had already survived a jail term *and* a drug overdose. If that wasn't cause for celebration, then I didn't know what was. And I did just that. I joined my friends back in the bedroom and snorted coke until the sun came up the next day. It was then that I received a text from Joey. It said that he needed to meet with me. He hadn't been at the party when I returned, but I learned that he *had* been there when I overdosed. I had no idea what Joey wanted to discuss with me, but I knew it couldn't be good.

Chapter 12

Joey had requested my presence at his townhouse in Northern Virginia for our meeting. That meant that I had about an hour's drive to think about all the different reasons for which Joey could want to see me. Everything from best case to worst-case scenarios played out in my head. Maybe I was moving up in the organization. Maybe Joey was going to surprise me and finally introduce me to Big Mike. Then again, I was just a day removed from overdosing, so maybe he was calling this meeting to terminate my employment. Then my mind began to race as to just how that would play out.

Would he simply let me know that things weren't working out and wish me well in my future endeavors? If so, would there be a do-not-compete clause I'd have to sign? You know, stating that I wouldn't sell any drugs in his territory for a certain amount of years? Then it occurred to me that this line of thinking might be a little too 'corporate.' If I were going to be let go, did I know too much? Would Big Mike's family be content to just let me walk away and hope I never got picked up by the cops again and decide to trade information on them for my own freedom? That's when the grizzly reality set in that this meeting could very well end with a handshake and a bullet to the head.

That was my last thought as I pulled into the parking lot in front of Joey's place. I took a deep breath as I turned the ignition off and headed toward his front door. Joey greeted me with a handshake at the door and invited me inside. I noticed right away that nobody else was in the house. This couldn't be a good sign. Typically, Joey would offer me a line of coke like a normal host would offer his guest a drink. There was no such gesture this time around. That couldn't be a good sign either. Joey asked me to sit down on the couch, and he took a seat in a recliner across the room from me.

"How are you feeling?" he asked.

"I'm good," I replied.

"You sure?"

"Yeah," I said, a bit defensively.

"You gave everyone a real scare last night. OD'ing is serious business."

"I know," I said. "That was a one-time thing. It won't happen again."

Joey stared at me as if it were up to me to continue the conversation. It became very awkward very quickly.

"I swear. It won't happen again," I continued.

"I hope not," Joey said, finally smiling. "We have big plans for you."

I felt a small level of relief when I saw his smile, but my

gut told me to stay on guard. "Great," I said. "Let's talk business."

"In a moment," Joey said, his expression now changing to a more serious one. "Big Mike likes what he sees from you. But 'made men' in this organization don't use drugs like you have been. Sure, we use, but not because we have to…because we want to. And we definitely don't abuse them. That's rookie stuff. If you're going to be one of us, you have to always be in control. Besides, you're still on probation. You have to be smart. If you test positive on any of your random drug tests, you can go straight back to jail. Do you understand what I'm telling you?"

I did and I didn't understand what he was telling me. To be honest, I kind of zoned out for a minute or so. It was the first time I heard the phrase 'made men' and as soon as I did, my mind started to wander. This was all I ever wanted…to be a 'made man' in a crime family. I would have the clothes, the money, the drugs and most of all…the respect I deserved. This wasn't a game anymore. I was now playing with the big boys, and there was no backing out. This was everything I had dreamed of for years. I was finally going to become a gangster. I know that's hard to wrap your head around, but it's true. Just like other teenage boys want to be a professional athlete or a fighter pilot or a doctor, this was my dream. And unlike most people my age…I was actually living it.

"Matt, do you understand what I'm telling you?" Joey repeated.

I immediately snapped back into reality. "Yes. Of course."

"Good," he said, smiling again. Then he went and retrieved a mirror from the other room and laid it on the coffee table between us and did a line of coke with me. I guess he felt he had to have the 'get your drug usage under control' talk with me before his conscience would allow him to get high with me.

Once Joey snorted his line, he leaned back in his recliner and smiled again. "Now it's time to get down to business. Like I said, Big Mike likes what he's seen from you so far. And I'm not just talking about your distribution. No doubt you're a great earner. But you've shown a lot more than just that."

I was now smiling too...from ear to ear. I had no idea where this compliment was heading, but I was enjoying every second of being in Big Mike's good graces. I was starting to feel like I may walk out of this meeting receiving a promotion instead of a bullet.

"Big Mike *and me* were both impressed with the way you handled yourself on the inside," Joey said, referring to my recent incarceration. "You did your time like a man. And it's not just the fact that you kept your mouth shut about anyone else. It's the fact that you never reached out for help from any of us. You stood on your own. And you stood tall. That doesn't happen often. And when it does, it should be rewarded."

I was now literally sitting on the edge of my seat on the couch. I would have been cool with Joey singing my praises for the rest of the morning, but I was also anxious to hear more about this 'reward.' Any trepidation I had about this meeting was now out the window. The fear was gone and the excitement had returned. This was definitely the life for me.

"Big Mike wants to put you in charge of his pill division. You will be responsible for all Oxy distribution under him. This means you don't just move Oxy in this area.

You expand your operation to the rest of Virginia. And Maryland. And Tennessee. Do you think you can handle that?"

He could have said Sri Lanka, Timbuktu and Narnia for all I cared. I would have found a way to make it happen. I could barely contain my excitement. My territory just more than tripled. And I'm sure that meant that my earnings just had too. I was moving up faster than I had ever dreamed possible.

Joey and I did another line of coke to celebrate the business deal, and he shared some more logistics of the job with me. I was now in charge of not only obtaining pills, but also distribution and collection. This was a lot like it was before, but I always had Joey to lean on if something didn't go right. Now, with this new job title, I was only to go to Joey with emergencies. Everything else, I was expected to handle.

Obtaining pills was the easy part. Joey introduced me to a few unscrupulous doctors in the Northern Virginia area who were happy to write scripts in exchange for a Benjamin Franklin slipped their way each time. I then found users who I would send in to these doctors' pain clinics to obtain the scripts. They would in turn get a few of the pills they just purchased with my money and everyone was happy. And best of all, I was never part of the actual transaction. I had learned this lesson the hard way. I started spending a lot more time on the road because of the expanded territory, but it was worth every mile I logged on to my odometer. Collections didn't seem to be a big deal. Most buyers knew who I was affiliated with and were happy to pay in full and pay on time.

This high-rolling lifestyle lasted for a full three days. Then the results of my latest mandatory drug test came back. I tested positive for cocaine and thereby violated my

---

probation agreement. If I had believed in God at this point in my life, I would have sworn He hated me.

Chapter 13

The fact that I was heading back to jail didn't bother me near as much as the fact that I had just compromised everything that I had been working so hard to build. Joey and Big Mike had been gracious enough to give me a second chance. I doubted their generosity extended far enough for a third.

It turned out that the lawyer my parents hired was able to use my dad's clout and reputation in the community to avoid any more jail time for me at this point. The only stipulation was that I had to check myself into a rehab facility to get help. I wasn't too thrilled about heading to rehab for thirty days, but it was the lesser of two evils. And maybe Joey and Big Mike would be a little more forgiving if I were sitting in group therapy sessions as opposed to sitting behind bars.

I reached out to Joey over the phone and explained my situation to him. He didn't sound too happy. He said he would speak to Big Mike and get back in touch with me. In the meantime, I found out that I would be a mandatory guest of Edgehill Recovery Retreat Center. It was located in downtown Winchester, so at least I would still be local. The center itself was a large brick building built in the 1800s with several additions that had been added on over the years to modernize it for the rehab clinic it is today.

Before I entered Edgehill, I heard back from Joey. He told me that Big Mike was concerned, but that he would reserve judgment on me and see how I handled business from within the treatment facility. "It has to be business as usual," Joey told me. This was going to be tough. I had to run my business from a distance. I wasn't big into absentee management, but I was going to have to make due somehow. And this wouldn't be easy, seeing as how cell phones were prohibited at Edgehill.

My first order of business was obviously sneaking in a phone. This wasn't difficult. I had one of my earners visit me the second day I was there and slip me a cell phone when no one was around. I used this phone to pass on instructions to three of my earners. I gave them the seed money they would need. They would now be making the trips to Maryland and Tennessee and try to keep my business afloat until my thirty days were up.

There were about twenty to thirty guests altogether. Some were here voluntarily. Some, like me, were not. I had three roommates this time around. We all shared one open-spaced room and a joining bathroom. Each of us had our own twin bed and dresser, and that was it.

We had our therapy sessions. We had arts and crafts. We had physical fitness time. In our free time, most folks walked down the street to the nearest gas station and bought cigarettes. Smoking was allowed outside the building, so that's where you would find most residents in their spare time. My first week was pretty smooth. Remember, this wasn't my first rodeo. I had the Hurst House to thank for that. Because of my time there, and also at Randolph Macon to a certain degree, I knew how the game was played and what I needed to do to fit in and not make any waves.

I fully engaged in group therapy sessions and opened up about my 'addictions' even though in my mind I wasn't addicted to anything. I even feigned empathy for the other group members when they would share. And I didn't stop there. When it came to arts and crafts, let's just say that the baskets I weaved would have brought in top dollar at Hobby Lobby. I addressed our instructors as ma'am and sir and made sure I was the role model resident they had been looking for. To me this entire stay was nothing more than a chess match. I had to always be two steps ahead of the folks running the show. They felt they could trust me, and this allowed me to sneak off and make daily deals with my smuggled-in cell phone.

After a week here, one of my roommates informed us that he was going home to Baltimore for the weekend and was going to bring back some of the best heroine money could buy. He took orders from several residents and headed for home. Leaves from Edgehill were earned and, despite my clean record, I hadn't been there long enough to earn one yet.

I had one week in the books, but I was starting to go stir-crazy. Business was holding steady, but I knew it would be that much better if I were actually on the outside making the deals happen instead of orchestrating them like some sort of third-party contributor. My earners met with Joey and dropped off his cut of the action that weekend, and I touched base with him to confirm he got paid. In all actuality, I really wanted the opportunity to blow my own horn and show him that we hadn't missed a beat financially. Joey confirmed that he was paid, but didn't seem overly impressed. He reminded me that this was week number one. I still had three more to go. He also let me know that the longer I was away from the day-to-day operations, the harder it would be to maintain what I had built. Okay, that wasn't the old "Atta boy! Way to go!" speech I had been hoping for, but I'd just have to take this one day at a time and find a way to make things work.

My roommate returned that Sunday with the product he had promised. After he made his deliveries to his other customers, he and I cut out a couple lines of heroine and snorted it in our room that night. It was a nice relief from the stress of the weekend call with Joey. And I was being smart about my usage this time around. I knew that heroine would only stay in my body for about three days. My next drug test wasn't until the following week, so I was safe.

As it turned out, not everyone was as cautious about when they decided to use. A few of my roommate's customers decided to snort their heroine before a group session. It didn't take long for the counselors to realize that these guys were anything but sober. And that's when things took a turn for the worst.

The Edgehill staff was smart enough to realize that the group therapy debacle was probably not an isolated incident and that drugs had somehow found their way on to campus. The ones who were busted that day were punished, but now the hunt was on to find out who else was using, and even worse, dealing. To weed out anyone else involved, an immediate mandatory drug test was announced. As soon as I heard this, I knew the jig was up. I would definitely be busted. This was bound to be strike three for me. Or four. Or five. Honestly, I'd lost count at this point. But I did know this: I was going to be in trouble with Edgehill for failing their drug test, the police for violating my probation (again), my parents for disappointing them for what felt like the thousandth time and most terrifying of all, Big Mike and Joey for jeopardizing my place in their family.

There was no sense in waiting around. I knew I would fail the test, so what was the point? Also, I didn't want to give anyone the satisfaction of coming to my room to inform me that I had, indeed, failed my drug test and that the authorities had been notified and were on their way to take me on a one-way trip back to jail. I lit up a cigarette in the outdoor common area and pulled out my cell phone. I didn't even try to hide the fact that I had a phone on me at this point. What were they going to do...kick me out? I called up a buddy of mine to come pick me up. I then went and packed my bag. Within twenty minutes, I was riding shotgun in my friend's car while looking at Edgehill in the rearview mirror.

I was now officially AWOL from Edgehill Recovery Treatment Center. I was in violation of my probation agreement. And once again...I was a man on the run.

Chapter 14

I had been a wanted man before, but not like this. I now had multiple probation violations that constituted a warrant for my arrest. I wasn't going to make the same mistake I'd made before by getting picked up for frequenting some of my regular stops. I packed a bag and skipped town. I headed to the only place I could think of to be safe...Joey's house.

At this point, Joey was unaware of my circumstances. But I was out of options. I was hoping he would show me some mercy and welcome me back to the family with open arms. When I arrived at his place with my travel bag, the look on his face told me he knew something was up. He invited me in, and I told him what had happened at Edgehill. To my surprise, he didn't seem upset...just the opposite. He seemed a little relieved.

"Does this mean you're going to be able to concentrate on business again full-time?" he asked.

"Absolutely," I said.

"Good," he replied. "Welcome back. I'm sure Big Mike will be happy to have you back too."

I didn't have time to dwell on the fact that I was now a fugitive or the fact that I didn't know if or when I'd ever get to see my family again. I had to get back in the game and make up for the time I was gone. Joey was good enough to let me move in temporarily and sleep in a guest room he had. I was grateful to him for that. And the arrangement worked out well. I would work during the day and then come home at night and get high with Joey. I was using more than I ever had before. But it was okay. I was with Joey, and he knew how to keep his usage in control. I was sure he'd look out for me as well.

The weeks turned into months, and my runs to Tennessee and Maryland became routine. I wasn't a rookie any more. I knew exactly what my job was, and the smartest way to handle any situation. I remember one of my regular stops in Tennessee. I always stayed at the same Red Roof Inn and asked for the same room. The room I requested each time had a window overlooking a Waffle House next door. I did this so that I could go there to get something to eat and still keep an eye on my room. Some of my customers weren't the most scrupulous people I'd ever met. And while I didn't think they'd try to rob me face-to-face, stealing from my room would be a definite option for them.

After about six months, my life basically consisted of traveling the tri-state area for drop-offs and pick-ups and partying with Joey. We were making more money than I had ever seen in my life. And just as quickly as we were earning it, we were spending it. It was nothing for us to roll out to Atlantic City for a weekend and drop over ten thousand dollars. We were by every definition of the word...high rollers. And we loved gambling, but we especially loved the horse track. That is where we'd lay down huge bets. If we won, great! It just meant more money to gamble with. If we lost, we couldn't have cared less. We'd just pull out the next wad of hundreds and continue betting.

We also conducted a lot of business deals with potential buyers and sellers at the horse tracks as well. Heck, if our business would have been the least bit legal, we could have written a lot off in taxes. But when you're not paying taxes, what's the point of a tax break? And it wasn't just the weekend excursions where we would blow money. I remember buying whole new outfits just because I didn't feel like doing laundry and washing what I already owned. I know that sounds extremely wasteful, and it was. But I also wasn't in my right mind a lot at this point in my life. Joey's and my drug habits were increasing each week. Instead of just getting high in the evenings like in the beginning, we were both using almost all the time. And after a while, it started to affect my business.

I remember one trip to Maryland that didn't go exactly as I had planned. This was one of my regular stops, but also one of the shadiest. I drove into a subsidized housing project where there was only one way in and one way out. If you ever saw the movie *Training Day,* you have an idea of what I'm talking about. It definitely wasn't the kind of place you would accidentally wander into and ask for directions. You'd probably never be heard from again. This place was so scary that it was one of several locations that I wouldn't carry all of my product with me. There was too great of a chance that I would be robbed or even killed for it. I would often separate my pills out and stash some in a drainage sewer nearby or in some bushes off the beaten path. I may have been crazy for choosing this career, but I wasn't stupid.

There were times when I would meet several clients at one location over the course of a couple of days. This was one of those times. With my drug habit running rampant at this point, I ran out of coke after a few days and desperately needed more. This meant venturing into the heart of the projects where only the most hardcore dealers and junkies resided. Normally, I would have steered clear of this kind of environment, but I needed a fix badly. I found a dealer who could get me the cocaine I wanted, but his price was more than I had on me. Yes, I had already spent most of my income from this trip on my personal drug habit. That's how bad it had gotten.

I was meeting with another one of my customers later that night so I knew I'd have money then. I asked him if I could have the coke now and pay him later. In hindsight, this was a ludicrous request, but again, I was desperate. The dealer asked me if I was packing. I told him yes and very slowly pulled out my 357 revolver to show him that I was. It didn't matter if I was doing business in an upscale neighborhood or a place like this, I always carried for my safety.

He told me that I could have the drugs and come back with the payment the next day. But in the meantime, he would hold my gun for collateral. I didn't like this idea. The gun was worth way more than what I was going to pay for the coke. And besides that, it was a gift from Joey when we had first started working together. In a weird way, it had sentimental value to me. But a man's got to do what a man's got to do. Especially when he's in danger of sobering up. I handed over the weapon, and he told me to be back at 9:00 the following morning.

I went out and got high with a couple of associates I had met in one of the apartment complexes and then met my customer later that night to make sure I got paid to be able to pay my dealer the next day. After my business transaction was over, I went back and crashed for the night. When I woke up, the sun was already shining through the opening in the shades of the dirty apartment floor on which I was lying. I looked at my watch. 8:52 AM. I had eight minutes to get downstairs and up the street a few blocks to get my gun back.

I flew down the stairs and tore up the street in a sprint that would have made Carl Lewis proud. With sweat pouring profusely off of me, I made it back to the street corner of our original deal. The dealer was already there with a few of his buddies waiting for me. Still breathing heavy from my run, I handed him the cash I owed him.

"What time is it?" he asked.

One of his buddies standing behind him answered. "9:02"

"It looks like you're late," the dealer said.

"Are you kidding me? I'm like two minutes late, and you're going to hold that against me?" I asked in disbelief.

"A deal's a deal," he said. "Keep your money. I'm keeping the gun." He held it out to admire it and to show it to me one last time while he gloated. "Do you need anything else?" Two of his buddies took a step toward me to show it was a numbers game at this point, and I was on the losing end.

As I drove home later that day without my gun or most of my payoff, I convinced myself that everyone has bad days. I would just chalk this one up to a teachable moment. I would take what I learned from the last few days, apply it to my life and come out of this an even better man than before. Little did I know that my best drug-dealing days were behind me.

Chapter 15

Well over a year had passed, and I was still living the good life. I now realize that "good" is a very subjective word to use. The life I was living included selling more and more pills as my customer base grew and staying on the run from the law. I definitely have a different definition of what the good life is these days than I did back then.

I was still living with Joey and had become the biggest earner in the family. Joey and I were bringing in an average of fifty thousand dollars per month. That's not too shabby for a guy without a high school degree and who wasn't even of legal drinking age yet. I often liked to think about what my former classmates were doing with their lives and wonder how much they paled in comparison to mine.

I had yet to meet Big Mike, which was a little frustrating at this point, but I noticed he was becoming more and more involved in our day-to-day activities. Several more meetings between he and I were scheduled and then cancelled at the last minute. Joey spent more time with him on the phone and would relay any questions or concerns that Big

Mike may have. He was a very cautious boss. It had been a few years now since I first met Joey and not only had I still never met the guy, but I had no idea what he even looked like. I wondered if the cops had that same dilemma. I also wondered if I had met him before without knowing. Had he ever been on the street watching me do business? Was he keeping personal tabs on me? The bottom line was that I didn't know. And I wasn't about to ask Joey. If Big Mike was keeping an eye on me, Joey's allegiance lied with him, not me. He wouldn't tell me the truth if I asked. And I didn't blame him for that. I admired the loyalty.

Despite our customer base growing, we were starting to have issues. Just like any growing business, there were going to be setbacks and obstacles to overcome. The first hurdle we encountered was that our doctors were starting to get a little skittish. At first, they were content to take their cash and supply the pills. But as our demand for oxy grew, they were getting nervous about how much they were supplying. The last thing they wanted to do was to call unwanted attention to their pain clinics. The pushback from the doctors came in some of them wanting more money for their troubles, and others simply wanting out altogether. The risk, in their opinions, had become greater than the reward.

We cut a few of the doctors loose and increased the fees for the others. The good news was that our out-of-pocket expenses stayed about the same. The bad news was that our market for obtaining pills was shrinking. This was a serious cause for concern. All of our eggs were starting to come from fewer and fewer baskets. Just like a solid stock portfolio, it's always good to diversify your assets. That way, if something drastic happens, you're somewhat insulated and avoid a catastrophic loss. At least that's what I've been told. The extent of my experience with the stock market usually consists of buying high and selling low. But when it came to the pain clinics we worked with, diversity was definitely good. Not only good, but also necessary. The fewer clinics we had, the more attention we could potentially draw from the authorities. And on top of that, if we lost any more, we wouldn't be able to meet our customers' demand.

If I'm being completely honest here, it wasn't just the customers' demand for pills that I was worried about. It was my own. Joey and I had slowly but surely increased our usage over the last six months to the point where one could argue that we were not just recreational users anymore. What started out as snorting a few pills per day grew into popping as many as ten per day. Then fifteen. By this point, I was taking at least twenty pills per day. And that was just to function. Sobriety and a clear mind were distant memories. To put this into perspective, I was spending ten thousand dollars per month on pills. Yes, you read that correctly. *Ten thousand dollars per month.* And that was just to get through each day.

I was no longer even enjoying Oxy, but I needed it. Normal, mundane activities became burdensome. Getting out of bed in the morning. Getting dressed. Interacting with other people. These were actually chores that I couldn't perform without the help of pills. And don't get me started on the toll it took on me physically. My body constantly ached. I felt nauseated more often than not. Chills and profuse sweating were part of my daily routine. And there was only one cure for it all. Yep, you guessed it. More pills. I remember sometimes waking up in the morning and actually being disappointed that I had to get up and face the day. But it was okay. I had something I could take for that.

So despite starting to lose some of our suppliers and not being the astute businessman I once was thanks to the Oxy, I managed to keep things moving in the right direction. It wasn't easy, and at times it felt like everything was on the verge of collapse, but I somehow managed to hold it together.

That is until a fateful drive on U.S. Route 66.

To this day, I don't know if it was the Oxy, the lack of Oxy in my system or just the fact that I had caught a bug that was going around, but I was sick as a dog. And to make matters worse, I was driving. Words can't describe how horrible I felt. Imagine the flu on steroids, and you start to catch a glimpse of how I felt. My body temperature would flip-flop from icy chills to a debilitating fever every few minutes. I couldn't stop sweating. My shirt was so drenched it looked like someone had just tossed me in a pool. My head was pounding to the point where it was hard to even concentrate on a single thought. I remember looking in the rearview mirror and seeing myself. You know that phrase, "Objects in the rearview mirror are closer than they appear?" Well, I got to see up close and personal just how bad I actually looked. My face was a ghostly shade of white that helped accent the giant dark bags under my eyes. If you've ever watched *The Walking Dead*, just know that I could have been an extra in one of their episodes.

Feeling as horribly as I did, all I wanted to do was get home and go to bed. So what do you do when you're in a hurry? Speed, of course. And that's exactly what I did. And that's exactly what the Fairfax County police officer pulled me over for. After I stopped on the side of the road, he walked up to my window and asked for my license and registration. I knew I was a wanted man and that my name would come back flagged if the officer ran it through their database, but at the time, all I cared about was not dying...yes, that's how bad I felt.

Sure enough, it only took a matter of minutes before the police officer knew that he had just pulled over a wanted criminal. He asked me to step out of the vehicle and then proceeded to search it. I didn't care. He wasn't going to find anything. And that brings us to another side effect of drug use. Your short-term memory isn't what it used to be. After a moment or too, the officer reached under the driver's seat of my car and pulled out Oxy and heroine. Once I saw the drugs, I remembered putting them there. But up until this point, I had completely forgotten about them.

So here I was. On the side of Route 66. A wanted fugitive. In possession of drugs. Deathly ill. And to top it all off, I remember I was wearing a fanny pack. Not one of my finer moments. But as I'd soon find out…not my worst either.

Chapter 16

I was taken to the Fairfax County police station for processing. I made my one phone call to my parents and then was escorted back to my holding cell. In the weakened state I was in, the cot I laid down on felt like a down-feather, king-sized bed at a five-star resort. I immediately fell asleep and stayed that way until my parents arrived a little over an hour later with our lawyer in tow. I felt better physically, but I was now starting to realize the gravity of my situation.

Even with a laundry list of offenses that now included not only forging prescriptions and violating probation, but possession of heroine and Oxy as well, our attorney was still able to work some magic, once again using my dad's status in the community, and got me a far better deal than I deserved. He had talked to the Commonwealth Attorney, and an agreement was reached that I would be released into my parents' custody while arrangements were made to enroll me in yet another treatment center. The plan was that while I was being helped, my sentence would be decided, and I would serve my time after being released from the treatment center.

My parents drove me back home to Winchester, thankful that I was safe and going to get some help. I, however, had other plans. On the way home, I texted a friend to meet me at my parents' house and drive me back to Joey's. I wasn't about to watch everything that I had built in the past year and a half come crashing down around me. And I certainly wasn't going back to a drug treatment center, much less jail. I'd been on the run before and was successful for well over a year. I could do it again.

I left my parents' house late that same night. I didn't even bother telling them good-bye. I knew it would break their hearts. At the time, I wondered if I might be putting them in jeopardy. After all, the police had released me into their custody. Would they be held responsible for my running again? Thankfully, it turned out that they were fine...I just added one more crime to my rap sheet.

I got back to Joey's in the middle of the night and told him everything. This felt like déjà vu all over again. It hadn't been too terribly long ago that I had to explain to Joey how the police had busted me and that I wouldn't be dumb enough to ever get pinched going forward. Now I was giving him the same spiel all over again. He didn't say much, but his body language told me that he wasn't taking this well.

He kept pacing back and forth in the family room, repeating the entire story that I had just told to him back to me. "What am I missing here?" he kept asking. He found it completely unbelievable that I would be free to go home with all the charges they had pending against me. I tried to explain that it was in large part due to my father's clout. Also, it was just temporary, until they found a rehab facility for me to enter, and then from there, most likely, jail.

He asked me point blank if I had copped a plea and made a deal with anyone. He wanted to know if I had dropped his or Big Mike's or any of our accomplice's names. I told him, just like the time before, I had not. I wasn't a snitch, and I would never betray the family. Joey continued to pace as he repeated his questions all night. He seemed to become more agitated as time went by. He also asked me several times who knew I was here. I told him that nobody knew anything. I hadn't done anything to jeopardize our business. Finally, he said he would have to call Big Mike and let him know what was going on. He told me to get some sleep, and we'd talk in the morning.

I went to my room, but didn't get much sleep. I considered myself part of Joey and Big Mike's family, but I wasn't feeling too much trust right about now. I'd been through this before with them, and everything turned out okay. Maybe I was blowing things out of proportion. But then again, maybe the last time was the only pass they were willing to give me. I stayed awake as long as I could, partly because my mind was racing over everything that had occurred over the last twenty-four hours, and also for my own safety. I finally drifted off to sleep only to wake up a few hours later with Joey standing over my bed, staring at me.

"Get up," he said. "You're coming with me."

"Where are we going?" I asked.

"You're going to help me take some trash to the dump. Let's go."

When I heard Joey mention the dump, all I could think about was the steel compactor unit and how it would have no problem smashing a human body. And how no one would ever even know the body was in there. And then how nobody in the world knew where I was right now...except for Joey and Big Mike.

We drove to the dump in silence. And it was deafening. I honestly didn't know if these were my last moments alive or not. I had lived with Joey for over a year, and this was the first time he had ever asked me to go to the dump with him. I thought about texting my family to let them know that I loved them, but didn't. We finally arrived at the dump, and Joey parked his truck and just sat there. There was an old man working at the dumpster that day. I was wondering if Joey was waiting for him to go inside, to give him an opportunity to whack me with no witnesses. After awhile, the old man walked behind the dumpster, and I held my breath.

But instead of pulling out a gun, Joey simply started to talk. "Things aren't good. We're losing more of our doctors at the pain clinics, and now you've brought the heat down on us even more. We can't keep doing what we're doing. Something has to change. I just don't know what it is. Big Mike's not happy either." Then he looked at me as a friend again and sincerely asked, "What are we going to do to fix things?"

I felt a sense of relief. For the first time that day, my life didn't feel threatened. I knew business was heading south, but it was nice to hear Joey ask me what *we* were going to do about it. It made me feel like I was part of the family after all. They say that desperate times call for desperate measures, and I had been carrying an idea around in my head for some time now. It was a last-resort type of plan, but it felt like we were all out of options at this point. We needed the cops off of our backs. We needed to rely less on the pain clinics and their shifty doctors. We needed to maintain our revenue, and we definitely couldn't afford to go without Oxy for a day.

I took my time and chose my words carefully before speaking. I knew that once I put this out there, there was no taking it back. I had an idea, and it was a game changer. This was bigger than anything we had ever dreamed of, much less carried out. It was high-risk, high-reward. It was an all or nothing plan. If we succeeded, we would be self-sufficient for a long, long time. If we failed, we would be in a maximum-security prison for a long, long time.

I stared at Joey for a moment before speaking. "I know what we're going to do. We're going to rob a pharmacy."

Chapter 17

After some discussion, Joey was on board, and our plan to rob a pharmacy was underway. We decided on a small pharmacy just outside of town. We drove by it several times and even parked and watched it to find out when it was busy and when it wasn't. We knew all the best roads leading into and out of the pharmacy. The only area where we fell short in our planning was that we never actually went inside the pharmacy to see how it was laid out. Remember, I never claimed to be a master criminal.

After a few days of planning, we were ready...or as ready as we were going to be. Joey was the driver, and I was the one who was actually going to go inside and rob the store. I wore two pairs of clothes that day. One pair to wear during the robbery and another pair underneath to wear after the fact, when the job was done. I had a mask and a fake gun with me. I decided to use a fake gun instead of a real one because I knew I was still not myself with all the Oxy I was taking and just wanted to make sure that nothing went drastically wrong. If there was no real gun and no real bullets, there was no chance of anyone accidentally getting shot. All I wanted was the Oxy. The last thing I ever wanted was to hurt anyone.

Joey parked down the street, and I exited the car and walked toward the pharmacy. It was as if someone had hooked an IV up to me and pumped double espressos directly into my bloodstream. The adrenaline rush I was feeling was like nothing I had ever experienced in my life. My vision was starting to blur, and I felt like I was going to vomit as I got closer and closer to the store. Suddenly I wasn't aware of anything around me. All my senses were honed in on the front door that I was now approaching. My hands were shaking as I slipped on my mask and opened the door.

Immediately, I saw a young girl stocking shelves to my left. She turned around to greet a new customer, but her smile turned to shock as she looked at me. For a brief moment, all I wanted to do was to run back out the door and forget I ever attempted anything like this. But it was too late. This was it. I raised my gun and pointed it at the ceiling. Even though it was a fake gun, I still felt uneasy about pointing it directly at anyone. "Hands up! Hands up! This is a stick up!" I shouted to her and to the other customers I saw in the back at the pharmacy counter. It's funny, but with all the planning, I hadn't even thought about what I was going to say when I got inside the building. "Hands up" was the first line that popped into my head.

I quickly headed to the pharmacy counter. There were three other customers who slowly backed away from me with their hands in the air. I walked up to the pharmacist in the window and demanded that he give me all of his Oxy. He and another gentleman behind the counter obliged and started putting all of the pills into a large bag. I couldn't believe my eyes. I had never seen this many pills before in my life. And I was no stranger to large orders. As I would find out later, by pure coincidence, we had decided to rob the pharmacy hours after they had just received a new shipment of Oxy. I didn't know it at the time, but I was in the middle of an armed robbery of half a million dollars worth of Oxy.

After the bag was filled and handed to me, I started to backtrack my way out of the store. Nobody was trying to be a hero. Everyone was cooperating and waiting for me to leave. I yelled at everyone to stay where they were and not to move. Then I looked out into the parking lot to make sure the coast was clear. It was, and I took off sprinting down the street to where Joey was waiting for me in the car. I jumped in, and he sped off. We didn't pass any cop cars or hear any sirens as we headed out of town. We got in and out just as planned and were now sitting on a half a million dollars of product.

My heart was still racing as I stripped off my clothes and threw them into a bag I had brought with me. I didn't want anything linking me to the robbery. Once the clothes were in the bag and unceremoniously tossed them out the window on the side of U.S. Route 66. The clothes were now a distant memory and nobody could link me to them.

We arrived back at Joey's house, and I was still shaking like a leaf. I had never done anything like that in my life and despite the generous payout, I never wanted to again. But this was just the first part of the plan. Just to play it safe, Joey and I decided to get out of town for a few days. Joey was going to take his wife and go stay with some friends, and I was going to do the same. We decided it was best that we not contact each other either. We would reconvene at his place in three days and move forward at that time. Joey gave me enough Oxy to get me through the next few days until we met up again and took the rest with him.

I bounced around Northern Virginia for a few days, crashing with different friends. I made up excuses about Joey having family in so I needed to get away for a few days to give him the extra room. The last thing we wanted was anyone getting suspicious as to why we weren't heading home. After the agreed-upon time was up, I traveled back to Joey's house. I hadn't heard much in the news about the robbery, so I assumed that was a good thing.

I arrived at Joey's but didn't see his car. I checked my watch. I was a little early, so I decided to just sit in my car and wait. Even though I had lived there for over a year now, it was still Joey's house, and the plan was to wait for him to get there. So that's what I was going to do. An hour passed. Then another. I thought about it and finally decided that it was safe to call Joey on his cell phone. It went straight to voicemail. I decided against leaving him a message.

Another hour passed. Night was starting to set in, so I figured it was okay to go ahead and wait for him inside the townhouse. I opened the door and walked inside. It was dark, so I flipped the light switch. Then I stood there in shock. I surveyed the whole room and tried to keep my composure. The room was completely empty. No couch. No chairs. No coffee table. No TV. The kitchen was the same way. No table. No dishes. The fridge was empty. I ran upstairs to my room. No bed. No dresser. The entire townhouse was cleared out.

This couldn't be happening. My first reaction was that Joey had double-crossed me and skipped town with half a million dollars worth of drugs. But that just couldn't be. Not after all that we had been through together. I just couldn't believe it. Then I took a moment to compose myself and realize what truly happened. Someone had recognized that Joey and I were both out of town and used this opportunity to rob us. That theory made much more sense. And it kept me from suspecting my only real friend just ripped me off.

I decided to try calling Joey again to let him know that

we'd been robbed. This time I didn't get his voicemail. I got a message telling me that this number was no longer in service. That is when the reality of it all set in. Joey and the drugs were long gone. And I would probably never see either of them again.

Chapter 18

For the next couple of days, I bounced around town, trying to score pills where I could with what little money I had left. I crashed at a different friend's house each night. The thought of Joey skipping town still didn't feel possible. But with each passing day, the reality of the situation became more and more real. My moods would swing from anger to confusion to disappointment. I was angry that he skipped town with the drugs that *I* stole. I was angry that he just flushed our entire business down the drain. And I was confused. *Why* did this happen? Did Big Mike orchestrate this? Was I being used the whole time? Or did Joey also skip out on Big Mike? Had he turned his back on the entire family? But the disappointment was the worst emotion of all. Joey had been like a brother to me for the last couple of years. He took me in, gave me a job and watched over me. In all honesty, he had been my only friend for a long time. I couldn't put a price on our relationship. But apparently he could. And that price was half a million dollars.

It didn't take long to realize that the gig was up in every sense of the term. I just went from a five-figure per month income to no income at all. I had no place to live. I couldn't support my drug habit anymore. I was physically ill because withdrawal had started to set in. Remember, I was used to snorting around twenty pills per day. Now I was lucky if I was able to bum one or two. And there were still multiple warrants out for my arrest. I had hit rock bottom and had nowhere left to turn. That's when I decided it was time to stop running and return to the only place I knew I could. I went home. I didn't even bother calling my parents. I just drove to their house. I wasn't really sure how I would be received, but this was my only hope. It turned out that they could not have been happier to see me. That's the thing about my family. It didn't matter where I'd been or what I'd done, they always welcomed me back with open arms. And I can't tell you what a fantastic feeling that was.

My parents agreed that I could stay at their house long enough to get myself cleaned up, and then we would contact our lawyer and come up with a game plan to turn myself into the authorities. I was ready to try and make amends, put my current lifestyle behind me and somehow try and start fresh. And besides, all I was wanted for was forging prescriptions, drug possession and violating probation. Thank goodness I was never linked to the armed robbery.

Getting clean was a much simpler concept in my mind than what it turned out to be. The next week of my life was by far the worst I'd ever experienced up to this point. Withdrawal is not a pretty sight. I remember lying on my bathroom floor, curled up in a fetal position, shivering like I was in a bathtub full of ice water. The physical pain was excruciating. It felt like every bone in my body was being slowly broken over and over and over again.

The pain never stopped. It just went on and on. I cried and screamed and begged for it to stop. The only time I stopped crying was when the pain was too much to bear, and

I vomited…which happened a lot. The suffering was also debilitating. Not to get too graphic, but I can't tell you how many times in that five day span that I lied in my own vomit, urine and diarrhea…unable and unwilling to move. I know you could have probably done without that last image in your head. But I wanted to paint this picture as accurately as possible. There are always consequences to our actions. And this was my consequence of years of drug abuse.

During this time, it was also incredibly difficult for me to function as a normal person. I had severe social anxiety in any interaction with my family. I couldn't eat anything without my body rejecting it. I remember eating nothing but soup during that seemingly never-ending week. I also had to take over-the-counter sleeping pills just to be able to fall asleep at night and temporarily escape the pain. I'd be lying if I told you I never thought about calling someone and scoring some Oxy during this time to make all the pain and suffering magically disappear. I thought about it a lot. But I'm proud to say I never acted on it.

Just like the famous phrase, 'This too shall pass' promises, my withdrawal did indeed pass. I remember my first full day of being clean and sober. I decided to watch the news because I just assumed that's what normal people did. I turned on the TV that morning just in time to see footage of an airplane flying into the Twin Towers. I stayed glued to the television for the next few hours watching the horrific events of that day unfold. It felt as if the drugs had kept my emotions buried deep within me for years, because all at once they came pouring out of me in a strong way. I felt anger toward our attackers, sorrow for our victims and pride in our country. Like every other American, I will never forget that day. But not only for what happened in New York and Pennsylvania and the Pentagon. September 11, 2001 is also what I consider my sobriety date.

The longest week of my life was finally behind me, and it was time to look ahead. I called my lawyer and let him know that I was at my parents' house and that I was now clean. I let him know that I wanted to turn myself in but wasn't sure the best way to handle it. I'll never forget this phone call because he didn't believe I was actually clean and sober now. After all I had put him through with the charges and subsequent probation violations, I guess I couldn't blame him for being skeptical. Finally, after I told him I'd come to his office right then and there to take a drug test to prove I was clean, he started to come around and accept that I just might be telling him the truth.

My lawyer informed me that he would reach out to the Commonwealth Attorneys from Frederick and Fairfax counties and would be in touch to let me know what the next steps would be. I had gotten clean and was preparing to turn myself in. I was actually feeling good about myself. For the first time in a long time, heck...maybe ever, I had taken responsibility for my actions.

A few days later, my parents were having some work done on the computer in their home office. I know this sounds like a random fact to throw in, but it was the computer technician that was sent to the house that makes this story worth telling. Her name was Katie. She was about my age. And she was gorgeous. At this time, I was a little socially awkward, still trying to rediscover who I was while not under the influence of drugs. Lucky for me, she wasn't shy. She struck up a conversation with me the first day on the job. And for the first time in a long time, conversation came naturally for me. She knew who I was and a lot of what I'd done, and it didn't seem to bother her. In retrospect, I think she actually liked my 'bad boy' image. This made it easy to be myself around her, and the transparency was liberating.

She worked on the computer for a few days, and I

would stay by her side, keeping her company while she worked. For my parents' sake, I hope she wasn't charging by the hour because she spent as much time talking to me as she did tinkering with their PC. I got the sense she wanted me to ask her out, but wasn't sure. After all, I was rusty at this sort of thing to say the least. She gave me every opportunity in the world to pop the question, but I kept dropping the ball. I'm not absolutely positive, but I think she may have even stayed an extra day, after the computer was actually fixed, just hoping I'd muster up the nerve to ask her out.

Finally, I psyched myself up and rose to the challenge. I convinced myself that even if Katie said no, the pain of embarrassment would be nothing compared to the pain that I had just gone through the previous week. So, as she was getting ready to leave on her final day, I asked her if she'd like to go out sometime. I remember being nervous to the point that my heart was beating so fast, I was afraid it was a withdrawal symptom returning. When the words finally came out of my mouth, I noticed that my voice was a few octaves higher than normal. But despite my nervousness, she said yes.

She said yes! I was ecstatic. Now what? Where did people go on dates? I hadn't been on one in years. I decided I'd take the gentlemanly approach and ask her where she'd like to go. I figured this would make me look considerate and at the same time eliminate any chance I had of picking the wrong venue for a date.

"Where would you like to go?" I asked. "Your choice. I'm up for anything."

"Anything?" she asked.

"Anything," I reiterated.

"Okay. Why don't we go to church this Sunday, and then we can grab lunch afterwards?"

I'd been in a lot of awkward situations in my life, but this might be number one. Church? Really? That was what passed as a date these days? I wasn't sure if God even existed, but if He did, I guarantee I wasn't welcome in His house.

Chapter 19

My first date with Katie was wonderful. There was just something about her that not only allowed me to be myself, but also made me want to be a better person. Sure, I daydreamed through the first part of the sermon, but little by little, I started listening to certain words and phrases that the pastor was using. And by the end of the service, I was hanging on every word he was saying.

If what he was saying was correct, Jesus loved me unconditionally. Not only in the general sense, as in John 3:16 (yes, even *I* knew this Bible verse at the time), where we're told that *"God so loved the world,"* but in a personal sense as well. Jesus loved me...Matt Hirschberg. No matter what I'd done, no matter who I'd wronged, He still loved me. And just as important to me at the time was the fact that as long as I accepted Him as my personal savior, I was forgiven as well. That was something that had been missing in my life.

After the service was over, Katie introduced me to the minister, Pastor Bobby. I remember meeting him for the first time. I don't remember exactly what was said, but I do remember his gaze. He had the most piercing eyes I had ever seen. It felt like they were staring directly into my soul. There is no way he could have known all the stuff I had done in my previous life, but it felt like he did. And he told me that I was welcome in the church anytime. I didn't realize how much that acceptance had been lacking in my life up to this point. And it felt amazing to receive it.

Even though that morning in church would turn out to be my only real date with Katie until I was locked up again, she and I still remained close. We would talk about God from time to time, and I actually started cracking open the Bible now and then. I knew that I had put my past behind me, but I wasn't sure what direction to head in. John 8:32 stayed on my mind and brought me comfort. "Then you will know the truth, and the truth will make you free." The Bible told me that Jesus is the way and the light, and these passages, along with many others, really started to resonate with me.

I began to feel that not only did I want Christ in my life, but also I really needed Him. I had nothing else to fall back on. I wanted His love. I wanted His mercy. I wanted His guidance and protection. And according to the Bible and Pastor Bobby, He wanted nothing more than to give me all these and more. I finally felt like I was on the path to picking up the pieces of my life and moving in the right direction. It was also comforting to know that I now had the Lord guiding me where He wanted to see me go.

Where He would direct me in the distant future remained to be seen, but I trusted Him. I already knew where I was heading in the near future. My lawyer had gotten back to me and let me know that he arranged for me to turn myself in and be sentenced to ninety days in Fairfax County Detention Center. But wait…there was more. This term was to be immediately followed by time spent in the Diversion Center, located in White Post, VA. The purpose of jail was punishment for my crimes. The purpose of the Diversion Center was to help acclimate me back into the community as a productive member of society. I don't know why, but the sentence that was handed down to me didn't bother me too much. Maybe it was because I had done time before, so I more or less knew what to expect. Maybe it was because ninety days is a much shorter sentence than I was expecting. Maybe it was because I knew Katie would be waiting for me when I got out. Or maybe it was just because I had a new peace about me since accepting Christ. Whatever the reason, I was able to keep an upbeat positive attitude until my term started.

My parents drove me to Fairfax and tearfully said their goodbyes as they dropped me off at the county jail. Katie had already said her goodbye back home and promised she'd write and come visit. I still maintained my sense of calmness during processing. I handed in my belongings and exchanged my clothing for an orange jumpsuit. It wasn't until the guards escorted me into general population that I realized I wasn't in Kansas anymore.

Fairfax County lockup was vastly different than what I had experienced in Frederick County. For starters, it became abundantly clear that I was a minority here. In fact the majority of the jail consisted of Hispanic gangs, such as MS13 and other rivals. I would later come to find out that around fifty percent of the inmates didn't even speak English.

There was also a lot less freedom than I had known in Frederick County. Yes, we were locked in our cells at night, but during the day...we were actually locked *out* of them. Whether you wanted to or not, and believe me...at first I didn't, you had to interact with your fellow inmates during the day. And don't get me started on the food. I know this may come across as nitpicking. By no means did I expect five-star cuisine in jail, but I did expect to at least be able to identify what was on my tray. More often than not, I couldn't.

Another characteristic of Fairfax County that differed from Frederick County was the inmates' behavior. In Frederick, there may have been a tussle between two inmates, kind of like the one I was in. These were usually harmless, didn't last long and were never brought to the attention of the guards. In Fairfax, I wouldn't go a couple days without seeing a knockdown, drag out fight between inmates. Sometimes it wasn't just one-on-one. Sometimes they were gang fights. To make the scenes even more chaotic, sirens would blow and a team of prison guards would rush in with their clubs drawn and 'handle' the situation. Thankfully, I never experienced any of this up close and personal, but just seeing it was scary enough.

My time there wasn't all bad. Just like my last stay, I was paired with a cellmate who turned out to be a good guy. His name was Don, and he was a Christian. I couldn't help think that God had blessed me with this guy. I remembered Proverbs 27:17, "As iron sharpens iron, so people can improve each other." I really think God put Don and me in each other's lives during this time to help us to remain strong in our faith and to lean on Him. We would request a Bible in the evenings and read it and study together. Through these times, I could feel myself growing even closer to the Lord.

But this wasn't the only reading I did while I was in jail. Keeping with the theme of trying to put my life back together, I was given the opportunity while serving my time there to go back to school. And that's exactly what I did. Fairfax County provided the chance for those who never finished high school to earn a GED. I decided it was time to do just that. Better late than never, right? I sat in a classroom with about thirty other inmates and basically went back to school for the majority of my stay.

I thought class would be a breeze, but once again, I was wrong. It wasn't that the curriculum was necessarily hard. It had just been a long time since I had sat in a classroom and actually studied. So I poured myself into the class work, diligently completed my homework and studied more than I ever had in my life. When it was all said and done, not only did I receive my GED, but I also graduated number one in my class.

God had blessed me with another success on my road to rebuilding my life. As my sentence continued, and my time started to wind down, days felt longer and longer. I knew it was because I couldn't wait to get home and see Katie again. Yes, I was heading to the Diversion Center after this, but I would be closer to home and would have a little more freedom to see her during this time. She came to visit me in Fairfax as often as she could, but it just wasn't the same.

I only had a week left before I was released when a guard approached me and told me that I had visitors, and that I needed to come with him. I found this odd because visiting hours were over. And besides that, I wasn't expecting anyone. I didn't know what this was all about, but my gut told me it couldn't be good.

Chapter 20

The guard walked me down to a holding area where I got to meet my 'visitors'. They turned out to be two United States Marshals. They were both well-built and stared at me like they wanted nothing more than the chance to beat a confession out of me. But for what? I had already turned myself in for my crimes. Maybe it wasn't personal. Perhaps the scowls on their faces were there because they were both just born without a sense of humor.

"Matthew D. Hirschberg?" the first humorless Marshal asked.

I nodded my head.

"We're taking you to Alexandria for questioning regarding a robbery that you were involved in earlier this year. Your cell is being cleared out, and your belongings are being packed as we speak."

I felt like my heart literally stopped beating. I started to stammer as I spoke. "B-b-but I 'm supposed to be heading to the Diversion Center next week."

The second Marshal smiled at me. "Yeah. You *were*." Then they looked at each other and chuckled. I guess they had a sense of humor after all.

I was allowed to change into my street clothes before we left. It was nice to finally wear something besides a green jumpsuit. I rode in the back of an official government van while my escorts sat up front. Neither Marshal spoke to me on the way to Alexandria. In fact, they didn't even say one word to each other. I found this very disconcerting, but it did allow me some time to process what was actually happening. How did anyone know about the robbery? Had Joey been picked up? Had Big Mike turned us in? Should I deny everything? These and hundreds of other questions bounced around inside my head for the remainder of the trip.

When we arrived at the Alexandria Detention Center, I had to trade my street clothes back in for a jumpsuit again. At least this time it was orange and not green. I know that sounds like a minute detail, but anything to change up the monotony was appreciated. To my surprise, I didn't meet with anybody that day. I was given one phone call to make, which I used to call my parents to get in touch with our lawyer, and then was taken to a holding cell and left for the night.

This gave my imagination even more time to run away with itself. Every worst-case scenario played over and over again in my mind. But I did a lot of praying that night too. And this helped give me a little peace in spite of what was happening around me. The difference between my situation now and my situations like this in the past, was that I now had a relationship with God. And I knew He would see me through this mess. God brought me to this point in my new life. I knew without a shadow of a doubt, He wouldn't let me regress now. I'd come too far.

Bright and early the next morning, a guard escorted me from my cell down a long hallway and into a meeting room. The room was relatively small with a large round mahogany table in the middle of it. In fact, the table took up about seventy-five percent of the room. I remember wondering how they ever fit this table in there to begin with. The walls were decorated with paintings of past Presidents and a few important looking documents. I recognized the Constitution as one of them. There was a distinguished looking gentleman in a suit sitting alone across the table from me. On the left and right of the table were other well-dressed men, about eight in all. Some wore ties. Some didn't. But they all wore button-down shirts and jackets. Finally, next to an empty chair right in front of me, I saw a familiar face…my lawyer.

My lawyer motioned for me to have a seat next to him, and he poured me a glass of water from the pitcher sitting in front of us. He put a hand on my shoulder as if to reassure me that everything would be okay. Then the man across the table from me turned on a tape recorder and spoke.

He introduced himself as a United States Attorney. He then went around the table and introduced everyone else. It turned out to be a pretty diverse group that was represented. Every three-letter law enforcement agency you can think of was accounted for. FBI, ATF, DEA…they were all there…to talk to *me*. The U.S. Attorney quickly set the tone of the room. He came across serious, but not at all hostile. Don't get me wrong, I didn't get the feeling we were going to be exchanging Christmas cards, but I didn't feel like I was being blatantly intimidated either.

"Do you know why you're here, Matt?" the U.S. Attorney began.

"No," I replied. I thought it best to keep my answers short and sweet until I had a better handle on the situation.

"Well, let me tell you," he said as he pulled out a file with my name on it. It was easily a few inches thick, which I didn't think could be good. He put on a pair of reading glasses and turned to the beginning of the file. And from there, he proceeded to read to me the most unbelievable story I had ever heard in my life. And not 'unbelievable' in the sense that what he was reading me couldn't really happen, it was more of 'unbelievable' in the sense that there was no way anyone could have known the details he was describing. And the U.S. Attorney read the story as if he were pitching a movie script to a Hollywood production studio. He was a fantastic speaker, and I would have been even more impressed had I not been trying to find a hole to sink down into while hearing the lowlights of my life listed, one after another.

In this government file were details of my life so miniscule that I had even forgotten about them. Not only did they know about the crimes I had already been busted for, but they knew details about them that were never previously revealed. They listed out every minor traffic violation I had ever had in my life. They knew about a time that I shoplifted a toy from Kay Bee Toys in the mall and returned it moments later when my parents found out what I had done. That was the level of detail on what they knew about me. They even knew intimate details about the pharmacy robbery as well…including that bag of clothes I threw onto the side of the road from the getaway car. Yep…that's how they linked me to the robbery. It wasn't hard. Barney Fife could have made that connection. After a quick DNA test on the outfit…I was their man. It turned out that I had been part of an ongoing federal investigation for some time now, and to say these guys were thorough in their work would be in the running for understatement of the year.

These folks at the table not only knew about me, they knew about everyone that I had done business with. Not only had the physicians at the pain clinics been busted in this investigation, so had Joey. He had been picked up in Tennessee. There was no mention of Big Mike though. I could feel myself starting to regress and want to plead the fifth if there was any way I could stay loyal to Big Mike's family. It was a weird dynamic. I was done with the drugs and the dealing, but I still wanted to respect that sense of family, and the loyalty that went with it.

The U.S. Attorney then told me that if I would confess to what they had just told me, that my cooperation would go a long way in reducing my sentence. I wasn't sure how to act. I was angry because I felt like I had been painted into a corner. I had also never turned on anybody before. Now I would be selling out Joey and the physicians that I had worked with. Even after what Joey had done to me, there was still a loyalty, not just to him, but also to Big Mike's family. Apparently, the U.S. Attorney observed my reservations and continued.

"First of all, Mr. Hirschberg, your family clout may have gotten you out of some jams in the past, but that ship has sailed. We don't care who your father is, or what he does for a living. He can't help you anymore. Furthermore, there is no honor among thieves. You may think you're doing the noble thing by protecting Joey's family. Well we've got some more news for you. You *are* Joey's family."

I looked up from the table and made eye contact with the U.S. Attorney, somewhat confused by his last statement.

"Now do I have your attention?" he asked. "You heard me correctly. *You* are Joey's family. *You and you alone.* There *is* no Big Mike. There never was."

Chapter 21

The U.S. Attorney continued to talk for a few minutes, but I didn't hear anything he was saying. All I could concentrate on was the fact that there was no Big Mike. This couldn't be true. I had just dedicated years of my life to the man, and now I was being told he didn't exist? My disappointment quickly turned to anger. Just then the U.S. Attorney slammed his hand down on the desk to regain my attention, and I immediately snapped back into the here and now.

"I'm going to tell you what's going to happen. You're going to give us a confession to confirm what we already know, or you're looking at a minimum of one hundred and sixty eight to two hundred and ten months in federal prison. And I'll make sure you end up in a hole someplace where we conduct all kinds of human testing you don't even want to know about. It's your choice. You can sit here and just stare at us with that dumb look on your face, or you can be a man and take responsibility for what you've done."

I remember three major points from the U.S. Attorney's

final comments to me. The first was that I think they propose your prison term to you in months as opposed to years because it sounds longer. But truthfully, fourteen to seventeen and a half years would have frightened me just as much as the monthly breakdown did. Second, I knew he was lying through his teeth about human testing. But that doesn't mean that it didn't scare me nonetheless. Finally, he challenged me to take responsibility for what I'd done. I had just started doing that in other areas of my life, and look where it had gotten me. Still, something about doing the right thing and owning what I had done in the past resonated with me. Whatever the consequences were, it felt right.

I looked over at my lawyer to see how he wanted me to proceed, and I'll never forget those two definitive words he spoke. "It's over."

I would have probably gone ahead and confessed and signed whatever papers they slid in front of me at that moment, but instead they decided to let me sleep on it. I was returned to my holding cell for the night to ponder my future. I spent another night in my cell praying to God. And by praying, I mean mostly yelling at Him. My emotions were all over the place that night. One minute I would be screaming at Him for not loving me, and the next minute I would be begging Him to help get me out of this situation. I told God I was through with Him forever, and then in the next breath told Him that He was all I had left. If He loved me the way I was taught He did, why was He letting this happen to me?

The prison sentence also weighed heavily on me that night. Regional jail was no walk in the park. I could only imagine the hell that federal prison would be. Even if I copped a plea, how long of a prison term was I facing? But as difficult to grasp as all of that was, the development that was hardest to come to terms with was the fact that there was no Big Mike and no crime family. How could I have not seen that coming? I wanted so desperately to belong that I let my judgment become clouded. Everything that I had worked to achieve in the past several years was literally for nothing.

Like clockwork, I was escorted from my cell to the same meeting room the next morning. All the same players from the day before were present. I nodded good morning to my attorney and took my same seat. The U.S. Attorney wasted no time in proceeding.

"What's it going to be?"

"Good morning to you too," I thought to myself. A few niceties wouldn't hurt.

"I'd give you a confession, but it seems like you already know everything," I said. It was a smug response, but I was just trying to salvage one ounce of dignity at my darkest moment. The U.S. Attorney didn't seem to mind, and I ended up sharing my side of the story and answering some direct questions from agents around the table. All of this was recorded, and the agents seemed to take copious notes as well. After the verbal confession, I signed a written one too.

My actual sentencing for these new crimes was several months away. Because of my cooperation, I had my bond reinstated and was free to return home to await my court date. I was under house arrest, but at least I wasn't going to be held in Alexandria until my sentencing.

It was great to be back home, out of jail and with Katie again. Sure, our dates all had to be at my parents' house due to my ankle monitor, but she didn't seem to mind. It wasn't the perfect situation, but at least there wasn't a thick layer of plexiglass between us anymore, and her visits lasted longer than fifteen minutes. It was wonderful spending time with Katie, but the thought of heading to a federal prison was like a noose around my neck, tightening with each passing day. Not knowing how long I was going to spend there only added to my uneasiness. I started overeating to compensate for my fears and anxieties. Food had definitely become my new 'escape' drug. When I was depressed about heading to prison, I ate. When I was feeling anxious about what could happen to a guy like me in prison, I ate. When I couldn't sleep at night, I ate.

Some people ask me how did I not relapse during this stage of my life and start using again to cope with what was going on in my life. The answer is simple. After experiencing what I went through in detox and getting clean, I have never once been tempted to try another drug. Simply put, the momentary pleasure is nowhere near worth the eventual pain. I was happy to substitute drugs with food. And my scales could prove it. I had gained sixty pounds in the course of a few short months.

Katie was so kind during this time. She would never come right out and address how far I had let myself go physically. But she would drop subtle hints now and then. She'd suggest we take a walk, which I'd shoot down and use my ankle monitor as an excuse. She'd suggest we have salad for dinner, which I'd shoot down because a couple double cheeseburgers just taste better. In hindsight, she definitely tried to help me, but it doesn't matter when someone doesn't want to help himself.

One of the few bits of knowledge that I remember from high school (before I dropped out), was that a body in motion stays in motion, and that a body at rest stays at rest. Never did I understand this scientific theory better than during this time. The more I ate, the bigger I got. The bigger I got, the less energy I had. The less energy I had, the less physical activity I was involved in. I was a big, fat body at rest, and that's all I wanted to do...rest.

It's amazing how similar the food path I was heading down was to the drug path that I had been down time and time before. The more I abused both, the more of a toll they took on my body. I remember times when I felt so bad about who I was when I was hooked on Oxy, that I would simply snort a few more pills to forget about the guilt. Now, here I was, picking up speed heading down that exact same road. But as much of a detriment that my overeating had been to my body, it had done its job of taking my mind off of my looming future in prison to some degree.

But my day of sentencing was coming. That was inevitable. When it finally did come, I had to buy a new suit to wear. No way was I fitting into any of my old ones. I was officially charged with conspiracy to distribute Oxycontin and robbery affecting commerce, for which the federal judge handed down a sentence of fifty months in Petersburg, Virginia federal prison. I remember wanting to cry, but tried to stay strong for my family and Katie. The most I had ever served was ninety days. And even then, I was released to Alexandria before the end of the sentence. How was I going to survive over *four years* in a federal prison?

I said good-bye to my family and Katie, was processed and taken away. Guards cuffed my wrists and ankles and escorted me and about a dozen other new prisoners onto a bus to take us to our new home. Nobody on the bus talked or even made eye contact with one another. We all just kept to ourselves, lost in our own thoughts. I was thinking about God and Big Mike…and how they were both now non-existent in my life.

Chapter 22

Once we arrived at the Petersburg Federal Correctional Institution, the first item on our agenda was intake processing. I had been through this process twice before, so I knew what to expect for the next week. The days consisted of various physicals and in-depth interviews. The interviews were a precaution to make sure that nobody had any gang affiliations. And if they did, they made sure they were placed a safe distance away from rival gangs inside the prison. At night, we would each be confined to our own cell. For a solid week, prison wasn't nearly as horrific as I expected it to be. I started to regain my swagger a little. After all, I'd been to jail before. Maybe prison wasn't so different. The whole 'been there…done that' mindset started to kick in. Then, after processing was complete, I graduated to general population. This is when the fun began.

The prison itself was a low-security facility, but originally it had been built as a high-security structure. That being said, some areas of the compound were more secure than others. The higher-security areas were used to house some of the more troublesome inmates. These inmates weren't necessarily higher-profile criminals. Most of them had been caught breaking the rules once inside and moved to these areas as disciplinary actions. So now that I've shared with you what these high-security areas were like and what kind of folks resided here, I'll give you one guess as to which area I was assigned.

That's right. I was the newest inhabitant of one of the disciplinary units in Petersburg. I was given a tote bag with soap, toothpaste, a toothbrush, a towel, a button-up shirt, khaki pants and steel-toe boots. Then I was escorted to what would be my home for the next fifty months. As the guard led me through the cell door, I quickly realized that I would not be sharing a cell with a single cellmate. I would be sharing a cell with every single person in this unit. The layout was a large, open-floor plan with bunk beds lined up on opposite walls. Each bunk had an accompanying locker behind it for the inmate's personal belongings.

I remember the overwhelming smell of cigarette smoke as soon as I entered the area. This was back when smoking was still allowed in prison. There was also a hint of sweet-smelling wine in the air. As I would soon learn, some inmates made their own wine on premises. There was a lot of yelling and the distinct sounds of dice rolling on the floor. I would also soon learn that dice, dominos and spades were the games of choice in here. I hadn't even arrived at my bunk yet, and I was sweating profusely, partly because I had never been this scared or nervous in my life, but mainly because it felt like it was one hundred and ten degrees in the place. There was no air conditioning only a few oversized fans placed strategically around the room. But all they were doing was pushing the body-odor-infused hot air around.

The guard dropped me off at my bunk and promptly turned and left. My new bunkmate who was already sitting on the bottom bunk looked at me and nonchalantly told me that I had top bunk. I nodded that I understood and proceeded to put away my belongings in my locker. The locker was nicer than I expected. Double doors with a shelf and hanger inside, protected by a padlock. So now that I was officially 'moved in', it was time for me to become acclimated to my new surroundings. Remember that swagger I mentioned earlier? Well, it didn't take long for me to realize that I definitely had *not* 'been here' or 'done this' before.

We were free to move around, but it was definitely a controlled environment. We were only allowed to move from place to place every hour. And when we did move, we had ten minutes to get where we were going. It reminded me of high school and getting from one classroom to the next between bells. There were a lot of options to choose from as to how you wanted to spend your days. Some of the different areas you could spend your time in included the chow hall, the infirmary, the yard, the commissary, the laundry room, the barbershop, the library, the recreational center and the chapel.

I kept to myself as much as I could for the first part of my stay. Needless to say, I didn't make a lot of friends at first. But that didn't stop the other cellmates from giving me a nickname. They called me Turtle. The name was chosen because I was overweight, had horrible posture and walked slowly. Did I love this nickname? Not at all. Was I going to tell these convicts to go back to the drawing board and come up with a better one? Absolutely not. I wasn't going to do anything to rock the boat or bring any undue attention to myself. Being a minority in prison felt like it brought enough attention of its own. The racial demographic at the time I was there was sixty percent African-Americans, thirty percent Hispanics and the remaining paltry ten percent was made up of white boys like me.

Another difference between regional jail and federal

prison I soon discovered, was that everyone works. Each inmate had a paying job. I started out working in the kitchen. And being the newbie of the bunch, I was assigned to the breakfast shift. What's wrong with the breakfast shift you may ask? Nothing at all…if you don't mind beginning your workday at 3:30 AM. But like I said, I wasn't about to complain about anything. My job would typically consist of cracking tubs upon tubs upon tubs of eggs. I would crack so many eggs that my hands would cramp up. But I mastered this skill set along the way. Even to this day, I can crack four eggs at one time…no shell. Okay, enough bragging.

Days were hard, but at least I had different environments and activities to help keep my mind off of not only being there, but being there for the next fifty months. Nights were much harder because that's when I was alone with my thoughts. I would lie in bed, knowing that there was no way I could do this for another four days, much less another four years. I would actually lie in my bunk and rub my feet together out of anxiety and nervousness to the point that I would literally rub holes in both socks and have to be issued a new pair.

And my mindset would get worse before it got better. One night, a female prison guard, who no one liked, was making her rounds through our area. A crew of five or six inmates, who were actually local guys from the Richmond area, decided they were going to put a little scare into her. These guys were wild and out of control and always pushing the envelope. Out of nowhere, they came running into the room, screaming at the top of their lungs. They each wore towels wrapped around their heads, looking like they belonged to the Taliban. They proceeded to set every trashcan on fire as they continued to wreak havoc by running around and knocking over everything that wasn't bolted to the floor. There was only one door for the female guard to escape through, and the Richmond crew knew this. Before she could reach her exit, they threw a bag full of every known bodily fluid and excrement you can imagine onto the door. The guard had to physically touch this mess to open the door and get out.

As she escaped crying, the prison alarms sounded, and a prison-response unit of guards came sprinting into the room. They were dressed in full riot gear, with shields and clubs. They were yelling at inmates and knocking over ones that were unfortunate enough to get in their way. Smoke was filling the air to the point it was becoming hard to breathe, and the sounds of grown men screaming were only eclipsed by the alarm sirens that were still piercing the air. With all the pandemonium happening around me, I will never forget lying in my bunk, curled up in a fetal position, holding a pillow over my ears and embracing a terrifying reality. *"I'm never going home."*

Chapter 23

Even though I was depressed and scared, eventually I started to make friends. I didn't go out of my way to do this, but relationships just started forming on their own. Being part of one of the disciplinary units, a lot of my fellow cellmates were what we referred to inside of prison as 'shot-callers'. These were guys who had connections and could make things happen. I'll give you a few examples. We had a bookie in our unit. Anything you wanted to place a bet on, inside or outside of the prison, this was the man you visited. We also had a 'weed & wine' guy. Anyone looking for pot or some homemade wine would go see this fellow. Interested in a new tattoo? You'd be in luck. We were home to the prison's finest ink artist, armed with a homemade tattoo gun with needles made from old guitar strings.

I don't know why, but most of these 'shot-callers' took a liking to me and watched over me. There was no motivating reason for them to like me. They just did. It was even suspicious to the guards that these inmates with clout would hang out with me. It reached a point where the guards were sure I was smuggling or hiding contraband for these guys, and would frequently pat me down to try and confirm this.

The 'shot-callers' were good enough to share their words of wisdom with me to help make my stay as uneventful as possible. There were certain rules you abided by in prison. And I'm not talking about the rules that were enforced by the guards. I'm talking about the unwritten code of conduct by the prisoners. These rules were to be followed either out of respect or for one's own survival.

One of the first rules was to never, under any circumstance, reach across someone else's tray from which he was eating. This was a blatant sign of disrespect. It was also the first brutal beat down that I witnessed in prison. One inmate reached across another's tray to grab a pepper shaker, and the first inmate promptly dumped the contents of his tray on the floor, and used it to beat the offender to a bloody mess until the guards broke it up.

Another sign of disrespect was to put anything on anyone else's bunk. This included your footprint. Breaking this rule was a definite cause for retaliation. Cutting in line was also not tolerated. Waiting in lines was a big part of prison. It felt like you had to wait for everything. We had to wait in line to be fed. There was always a line to do laundry, or to grab a seat at the barbershop. I remember waiting, on average, two hours just to use the phone. Line cutting didn't occur often, but when an individual did break this rule there was a good chance it was the last time he'd do it.

Other rules were simply survival skills. For example, whenever you sat down on a toilet to use the bathroom, you never dropped your pants below your knees. This was a prime opportunity for someone with a beef with you to jump you. And if your pants are below your knees, it's a lot harder to defend yourself, or even fight back. This next rule may sound crazy, but we always wore our steel-toe boots to the shower. That's right...grown men walking to the shower room, and all we were wearing were boots and a smile. We'd remove them during the actual shower, but then we'd put them right back on to wear on the way back to the locker room. The reason for this is that if you weren't wearing your boots, this was a perfect place for someone to jump you. It would be hard to keep your balance with your bare feet on a wet floor, so you'd automatically be at a disadvantage.

Yes, these 'shot-callers' watched out for me. But some of them also wanted to make sure I remembered the pecking order here in the big house. This led to my first altercation, and I remember it vividly. I was in the laundry room transferring my clothes from the washer to the dryer when the tattoo artist and a buddy of his walked in behind me and shut the door. It was a small room to begin with but suddenly felt a lot more confined.

The tattoo artist smiled a very unnerving smile at me while his friend whipped out a razor. My mind started racing. This was it. I was right. I was never leaving this place. I was going to die a horribly violent death right there in a prison laundry room. I thought these guys were my friends.

"We're going to shave your head," the tattoo artist declared.

"*You're going to what?*" I thought to myself. Granted this was definitely a step up from being murdered, but I wasn't about to let either scenario play out without some sort of a fight. I knew exactly what they were doing. They wanted to establish dominance. They wanted to find a way to remind me that they were in charge, and I was somewhere below them on the food chain.

The tattoo artist grabbed my arm and slid behind me, holding me in a bear hug and pinning my arms to my sides.

His accomplice moved toward me with the razor, and out of desperation I managed to kick it out of his hand. He quickly rallied and grabbed me from the front, sandwiching me between my two assailants. I was able to free one of my arms and grab hold of the guy facing me. The three of us stayed tangled and bounced off of the washing machine and then into the door. The doorknob buried into my hip, causing a deep-tissue bruise. The door flew open and left us in plain sight of a nearby guard. We promptly released each other and waved to the guard to let him know that everything was okay.

Relationships were different in prison. You have to be able to stand up for yourself but also show respect when needed. Had those guys shaved my head, who knows how bad my life would have become? Others would have seen me as an easy target and tried to establish their dominance over me as well. But by standing up for myself and pushing back, those guys never tried another stunt like that with me again. The key was not to go looking for trouble, but to be ready for it if and when it found you.

Birthdays were interesting experiences too. The birthday boy would always get a nice beating from his 'friends'. The rule of thumb was typically one punch for each year you were celebrating.

All the while, I continued to gain weight. I wasn't gaining as drastically as I had at home, simply because I didn't have access to the food that I once did. But the weight gain continued nonetheless. My family and Katie would visit and write as much as they could. And as great as it was to see and hear from them, it also reminded me of what I was missing on the outside, and that just continued to fuel my anxiety and depression.

It actually escalated to the point where I was having severe chest pains. This led to a series of tests at the prison infirmary. I had everything from a stress test to a colonoscopy to try to determine what was wrong with me. One doctor thought I was suffering from a leaking heart valve. It was finally determined that there was nothing physically wrong with me. All of my symptoms were being triggered by my nervousness of being in prison. And the only way to change that was to try and change my attitude about being there. And I couldn't see that happening anytime soon, if ever.

One memory I'd like to forget but never will, was my first Christmas spent on the inside. Do you remember what a big deal Christmas was for me growing up? Well, except for the one I spent in the Hurst House, of course. It was just the opposite in prison. First of all, there were no decorations. I can understand not having an actual tree, but not even a wreath or any flashing lights? No stuffed Rudolph or Frosty? The guards could have at least worn Santa hats with their uniforms, right? In fact, the only way you'd even know it was the most wonderful time of the year was that we were given a nicer dinner than usual. Depressed does not even begin to describe the way I felt that first Christmas in Petersburg. But what depressed me even more is the thought that kept running through my mind as I ate our special dinner.

"I have three more Christmases like this before I leave here."

And that may have very well been the most depressing moment in my life.

Chapter 24

It would have been easy to denounce God and my newly found faith after being sentenced to prison. And I'd be lying if I said I never thought about breaking up with Him. At times, it felt as though He had turned His back on me. But the truth is that once I was behind bars, He's all I had left. I found myself needing Him more than ever. All prisoners had access to Bibles, and I studied mine diligently. I also made note cards with my favorite Bible verses written on them. When times were tough and I didn't feel like I could carry on, I'd find somewhere private, usually a bathroom stall (pants above knees of course), and read one of them. I still remember all of my note card verses and have them memorized to this day. Here are a few of my favorites:

2 Timothy 2:7 "God did not give us a spirit that makes us afraid but a spirit of power and love and self-control."

Isaiah 41:10 "So don't worry, because I am with you. Don't be afraid, because I am your God. I will make you strong and will help you; I will support you with my right hand that saves you."

Philippians 4:13 "I can do all things through Christ, because He gives me strength."

In retrospect, I think God used prison to help me realize that I needed to rely completely on Him and not myself. Finally accepting this fact helped me through a lot of rough days. But none was as devastating as the day I received my very own 'Dear John' letter. I should have seen it coming. Katie's visits were becoming fewer and further between, as were her letters. And let's be honest…we had only ever gone on one real date.

It was hard enough as it was to read the letter, but the fact that it was so cliché definitely didn't help matters. I swear it was as if she had Googled 'Standard Break Up Letters' and copied and pasted the search result verbatim. If this *were* the case, at least she remembered to change out the name to at least make it appear to be personal. The letter included every standard break up line, including 'It's not you…it's me' as well as everyone's favorite, 'We just need some time apart.' *Really? Time apart?* I was in prison a hundred and fifty miles away. I honestly don't know how much more apart we could have been.

Hey, I know it wasn't fair to ask her to wait for me for four years. But it didn't stop me from sinking into a deeper depression than the one I was in already. My health continued to deteriorate while my weight gain continued to increase. At the rate I was going, I would never see the light of day again. At one point, I probably had a better chance of having a heart attack or stroke than walking out of prison a free man. But I found out that God wasn't finished with me yet. Throughout my stay, He had not only kept me safe, but had placed me with the right people who showed favor to me. There was no logic to why certain 'shot-callers' or prison guards took a liking to me and watched over me, but they did. And I have to believe this was God showing me grace.

One of the folks he made sure crossed my path while in prison was a guy named Roscoe. My bunkmate introduced me to him, and I liked him immediately. Roscoe had a lot of clout on the inside, and the other inmates respected him. He was also a Christian, and we ended up spending a lot of time together in Bible studies. He was very knowledgeable and encouraging during these times. In fact, to this day, Roscoe is one of the top three most inspirational people I have ever had the pleasure of meeting in my life.

Roscoe was also a dedicated weight lifter and a former personal trainer. You could find him and his crew spending most of their days on the yard at the bench press. And their time there paid off. It was nothing for Roscoe to bench press over five hundred pounds. I remember after one of our Bible studies, he asked me if I'd ever thought about working out. That was Roscoe's style. He didn't say, "Hey man…you look like death warmed over. You really need to start taking care of yourself." He simply planted a seed and let me decide if I wanted to pursue his suggestion or not.

Like everyone else, I had a lot of respect for Roscoe. So when he suggested that I work out, I decided to take him up on his offer. The very next day, I walked up to Roscoe and his guys outside on the yard at the bench press. This was a big deal because you had to be invited to join a crew to lift weights. Sure, technically I was never invited, but with Roscoe, I just assumed it was implied. Well, you know what they say about assuming…

It turns out that they weren't ready for me to join their group just yet. "We don't want quitters out here with us," Roscoe told me. "You need to prove to me that you're serious about wanting to get into shape before we let you in."

"I am serious," I assured him. "What can I do to prove it to you?"

"Start by walking the track," he said. "Then we'll see if you've got what it takes."

"No problem," I said. "How long do I have to walk the track before I can come back? Thirty minutes? An hour?"

Roscoe looked at me and smiled. "Ninety."

I looked back at him in disbelief. "You want me to walk the track in the shape I'm in for ninety minutes?" I asked.

"Ninety *days*," Roscoe said. Then he turned his back on me, signaling it was time for me to go.

Ninety days? Was he out of his mind? I would have to walk the unkempt, gravelly dirt track each day for three months? And for what? The *chance* to join their group? I thought about just going back to my bunk, but the sad truth is that I had nothing else to do. So I started walking. Each day I'd walk for hours at a time. Days turned into weeks. Weeks turned into months, and before I knew it, I had walked for ninety straight days. And my prison slacks started to become baggy. I had to tighten up my belt by a few holes. I also had more energy and started to feel a little better about myself.

True to his word, Roscoe let me join their group, and I started lifting weights with them on a daily basis. I continued to walk the track a lot too. I stuck to this regimen religiously for the next year and lost a total of one hundred pounds. I felt amazing. I had forgotten what it was like to be in shape and to have this much ambition. And it wasn't like I was working hard to earn these results. I actually enjoyed getting healthy. The walks on the track gave me time to reflect on the days past and plan for the days ahead, as I took care of my cardio for the day. I learned to alternate focusing on different muscle groups on different days for optimal results. And it was great camaraderie with the other guys at the same time.

That's why I jumped at the chance when I saw an opportunity for a certification program tacked on our community bulletin board. The prison was good about offering all kinds of programs, but I never paid too much attention to any of them. This time was different. There was a class being offered by the National Federation of Professional Trainers to become a certified personal trainer. I knew right then and there that this is what I wanted to do with the rest of my life. I wanted to not only be a certified personal trainer, but I wanted to one day own my own gym.

I shared my plan with Roscoe and his crew. Like always, Roscoe was completely supportive of my planned initiative, but some of the others weren't. There was one guy named Juice. He was a fifty-year-old ex-body builder who also happened to be our resident know-it-all when it came to anything having to do with weight lifting or gyms. He assured me that just starting out the way I had and being a complete novice to the industry, I'd never pass the certification program, much less own a gym.

Juice's negativity was not about to get me down. I signed up for the program and poured myself into it. Late night study sessions, classroom participation, you name it. I ate, slept and breathed this class and loved every minute of it. After six months, I was an official certified personal trainer. And the cherry on top...I ended up tutoring Juice to help him pass as well. Juice was wrong about me not passing the class, and I was sure he was going to be wrong about me owning a gym one day. For the first time in a long time, things were going my way. I was healthy again and had a plan for my future. Now all I had to do was finish my prison term and head home. Little did I know that there would be a significant detour along the way.

Chapter 25

It was September, and my release date was at ninety days and counting. I was excited to finally return home, but I was even more excited at the timing. I was going to arrive home during the Christmas season and would soon be enjoying my first Christmas with family in years. I could practically taste the eggnog and cookies. But it seemed that life had one last punch in the gut to throw me.

Whenever an inmate's term is coming to an end, he is assigned a counselor to meet with and help establish an action plan for life on the outside. Three months prior to my release date, I was given mine. At our first meeting, we talked about expectations and adjustments that may need to be made in my life once I was free. It was a good discussion until the very end. As I stood up to leave, he began with, "Oh…just one more thing."

In my experience, nothing good ever follows those words. This time was no exception. My counselor looked in a file and continued to talk to me without looking up. "It appears you were convicted of a couple possession charges in

Fairfax County. Is that correct?"

"Yes sir."

"Well, it looks like you were supposed to serve time at the Diversion Center as part of your sentence, but you never did."

"That's right. Because I was brought *here* instead."

"Be that as it may, you may or may not need to complete your time there. Fairfax still has a detainer on you, so upon leaving here, you'll be transferred back to Fairfax County jail for holding until a judge decides your future."

Had I been in the poor shape I was just a few short years before, I would have probably had a heart attack right then and there. I had done everything asked of me. I had served my time. It wasn't my fault that I was taken from Fairfax prematurely. And because of this oversight, I now had a chance of missing my fifth Christmas with family in a row. That was the scariest part. Not necessarily the 'missing Christmas' part, although that would be horrible. The scariest part was not knowing how long I was going to remain in custody until a judge got around to hearing my case. It could be days. It could be weeks. Or it could be months. I was at their mercy.

Needless to say, this made the countdown to my release from Petersburg somewhat anticlimactic. Sure, I was leaving prison…but I was going right back to regional jail. But not before my friends gave me a going-away present. I was sitting on my bunk when I saw Roscoe and about five of my other closest friends meandering toward me. The smiles on their faces told me exactly what they had in mind. Before I could make a run for it, Roscoe had me in a bear hug and threw me to the ground with all of his massive weight on top of me. Pinned to the ground, unable to move, the other five inmates took turns pummeling me. They were kind enough not to hit me in the face, but my stomach and kidneys paid the price. Like I said before, this was a ritual on the inside. It was your friends' way of saying, "We love you…but don't do anything stupid to end back up in here again. In case you ever forget how bad it is on the inside, this beat down is one final reminder." And as friendly as it was, there was no pulling any punches. They gave it all they had. After a few minutes (which felt like a few hours), Roscoe put me out of my misery by calling off the hounds. Then he pulled me up, smiled, and told me that he never wanted to see me on the inside again….and the feeling was mutual.

The next day, I shipped out and traded in my tan button-down shirt and slacks for another green jumpsuit, and I was back in Fairfax Jail for an undetermined length of time. It was amazing how different this place was the second time around, especially after spending the last four years in a federal prison. It was like returning to elementary school from high school.

In prison, most everything operated on a mutual level of varying degrees of respect. This wasn't the case in regional jail. I quickly had to learn to just let certain things go. Inmates would reach over one another's trays at mealtime. They would cut line in front of others, and there was little to no respect given to others' personal property. Each of these was a cardinal sin on the federal level, but not here. And I didn't want to call any attention to this, or especially to myself. I just wanted to serve my time and go home.

About thirty days (along with another Christmas) came and went, and it was finally time for a judge to hear my case. My attorney did a fantastic job representing me (again), and the judge ruled that my time had been served in its entirety. I was finally free to go home. I remember not fully believing it would happen this time until my parents actually drove me off of the premises. Then I remember smiling the entire way home.

I went home and slept like a baby that night in my own bed. It was the best feeling I'd had in a long, long time. The next morning, my mom served up a homemade breakfast, and I ate with the entire family. It was the perfect way to start the first day of the rest of my life. After woofing down a delicious meal and catching up with everyone, I started in on my to-do list. My first task was to buy new clothes. I literally had nothing to wear. I would have swum in any of the 'big and tall man' clothes I had hanging in my closet. I headed into prison weighing about two hundred and eighty pounds and now a hundred of that was missing.

My parents took me shopping, and I bought an entirely new wardrobe. Only this time, I was going to dress like a normal person. There would be no tight suits, no gaudy gold chains or pinky rings, and definitely no fanny packs. The next stop on my list was the DMV to obtain a new driver's license. I had surrendered mine upon entering prison, and it was never given back.

You think you've had bad experiences at the DMV? Try going there to apply for a new driver's license with no identification, no credit, no bill with your name on it, no current or former address to show and no job for the past ten plus years. It's very difficult to prove you are who you say you are. It was as if I had been completely removed from life's grid. At least the lady at the DMV was very friendly and accommodating to my plight. I'm kidding! It's the DMV. They couldn't have cared less about my problems. Finally, they took pity on me and accepted my birth certificate as proof of existence and issued me a new license.

My last stop of the day was to check in with my

probation officer. Her office was in Harrisonburg, so it was a two-hour round trip whenever I had to see her. It was only once a month, so it wasn't too hateful. And I had a good relationship with her, so the trips weren't bad at all. She did inform me that I was expected to have or have proof of trying to find a job within ninety days. I told her this would be no problem and shared my plan of working in and then some day soon, owning my own gym.

She smiled a sympathetic smile, but something told me that she felt the same way as Juice. I would never own my own gym. I smiled back, shook hands and left her office. It was okay that other people had their doubts. In their defense, why should anyone have believed I could own a business? I hadn't done anything to prove that I could. I was fine with others doubting me at this point. I just knew that I couldn't start doubting myself.

Chapter 26

The next day, I started beating the streets looking for a job. I applied to every gym in town and the surrounding areas. It was definitely disheartening to have to check the 'yes' box next to the 'Have you ever been convicted of a felony?' question on each application. Nevertheless, I kept my head held high and truly believed that one of these gyms would call me back and offer me a chance to come work with them. So I waited. And waited. The good news is that after a week, calls started coming in. The bad news is that they were all to tell me that they would not be hiring me. They didn't come out and say that it was because of my criminal past, but I could tell in their tone that it was definitely the reason.

I can't say that I blame them. I had no work history. There were no references they could call. I couldn't very well list Roscoe or Juice on the application. All I wanted was a chance to prove my worth, but I understood that was a big request, and as it turned out, not a very realistic one either.

Not being able to find a job and its negative effect on my self worth wasn't the only issue I had while adjusting to life on the outside. After four years away, I was finding it difficult to adjust to the real world. Everything seemed to move so fast. When I was in public, I felt like I couldn't keep up with life's pace. Then, when I was home, I didn't know what to do with my time. I was so used to having a schedule to follow for the entire day. It's hard to explain, but I felt like I transitioned from having no freedom at all to too much freedom to handle.

I also found myself becoming easily frustrated with the lack of respect I witnessed on the outside. The way in which I saw children or youth speak to adults was appalling to me. Common courtesy seemed to be in short supply. While prison had taught me to be grateful for what I had, there seemed to be a sense of entitlement in a lot of folks I met, and I don't think that is something that I would have ever picked up on before. I also had a difficult time accepting when someone cut me off in traffic, or drove past a long line of stopped cars to try and cut in front of everyone else already waiting. In my mind, that was the driver's way of saying, "My time is more valuable than yours. You can wait. I don't have time for this."

It wasn't just the little nuances I was picking up on in other people. I could tell that I had changed as well, and it was hard to break old habits. At dinner, I would ask my parents if I could have seconds instead of just reaching over and putting some more food on my plate. I never went as far as to ask permission to go to the bathroom, but I'm sure the thought crossed my mind inadvertently from time to time.

Throw in some anxiety and nervousness in certain social situations and you get somewhat of an idea what this adjustment period was like for me. And I'm not the only one. Lots of former inmates have a hard time making it on the outside. In fact, many of them end up returning to prison because it's more comfortable for them. I had no intention of going down that road. I was a free man, and I was going to learn to adapt. I was never going back. I didn't need to think about Roscoe's 'going away' present to remind me of how much better I had it on the outside.

My time to find a job was winding down, and I had exhausted all of my options for working in a gym. My parents were finally able to pull a few strings and get me a job working on an assembly line in a local factory. It wasn't my dream job, but I definitely needed work. I needed it to appease my probation officer, and also because I needed to earn my own money. So I accepted the job and began manufacturing filters. I would work ten hours straight, with two regularly-scheduled, fifteen-minute breaks and a thirty-minute lunch. And I was doing this all for minimum wage. This was a far cry from being my own boss and pulling in fifty thousand per month, but there was something to be said for good, honest, hard work. And it was legal, so that was a nice bonus too. I'll never forget the satisfaction of receiving my very first paycheck and how incredible that felt...until I learned what FICA was and how it affected my gross profit.

I took pride in my work there, and I gave it everything I had. I hadn't given up on my dream of owning my own gym, but with each passing day, that dream seemed a little less tangible. Maybe this was my lot in life. Perhaps this is where I was meant to be for my remaining days. It could be worse. Then one day, I was reminded of the importance of chasing your dreams.

Out of the blue, there was an unscheduled break, and we were all summoned to the main floor. Someone from upper management whom we rarely saw in the factory stood in front of us and called a woman from the assembly line to stand next to him. He introduced her to us (although I'm sure we knew her better than he did), and let us know that she was retiring from the company at the end of the week after giving them forty years of service. He thanked her for her time and gave her a watch as a retirement gift. We all clapped, and then a whistle promptly blew, letting us know it was time to get back to work.

That scene has stayed with me ever since that day. This woman had given her entire working life to this company, and she was rewarded with a five-minute break and a watch. Now I don't believe the company owed her anything, and it was truly a nice gesture, but it did remind me that I wanted something different out of my career. There is absolutely nothing wrong with factory work. It's a noble job, and I know some folks that wouldn't be able to cut it doing what these workers do. It's just that I felt I was being called to do something else. I was at a crossroads again in my life. I could take the easy road, stay on the assembly line and accept this as my fate, or I could continue to chase the improbable dream of being a gym owner, even though I couldn't even get an entry-level job working in one.

Unlike so many other times in my life when I was faced with a life-changing decision, this time I finally made the right call.

Chapter 27

I figured that if I couldn't get a job in a gym, it would probably be a good idea to at least *join* a gym. That way I could be close to those in the industry and hopefully something good could come of that. I had learned a thing or two over the years about the company you keep, and how it starts to reflect who you are and what you value most. And besides, I needed to get back to working out the right way. My little brother's makeshift bench press and my parents' hydraulic rowing machine in their basement just weren't cutting it for me. Even with Eminem's "Lose Yourself" blaring from the CD player, pumping me up, I needed something more.

After work one day, I stopped by a new gym that had just opened. I joined, and the owners gave me the grand tour showing me all they had to offer. Through casual conversation, it came up that I was a Certified Personal Trainer. They seemed to be impressed and offered me a deal that I didn't see coming. They told me that if I cleaned up around the gym and helped show customers how to use the equipment, they would waive my membership fee. They never asked me to fill out an application. They never specifically asked me if I was an ex-con. And I decided not to offer any of this information on my own. I didn't want to jeopardize this opportunity. I would get to work out for free *and* get my foot in the door, doing something I loved (showing customers how to use equipment…not so much the janitorial work).

And that's exactly what I did. Each morning I would drive to work. After my shift, I'd go home to grab a quick bite to eat. Next, I'd head to the gym to work out, help other customers and clean up. Finally, I'd come home at the end of the evening, go to bed and start the same routine over the next day. I was busy from morning to night, but I was making money at my real job at the factory, and I was moving closer to my goal and doing what I loved in the evening. This schedule continued for about four months.

Being a new gym, the owners had hired a gym-based consulting firm. The business was owned by a gentleman named Jeremy Wright. Jeremy ended up spending a lot of time on-site, training folks and helping to get things up and running. During this time, I got to know him pretty well, and we established a favorable relationship.

I'll never forget the first time our relationship hit its first bump in the road. I was walking into the gym one evening to start my workout and passed a family friend leaving the gym. We exchanged pleasantries, and she went on her way. As soon as I saw Jeremy, he asked if we could talk. That didn't sound good. It became even more evident that he wanted to talk about something serious when he led me into his temporary office and closed the door. He told me that he had just had a very pleasant conversation with the woman I had just passed. She had spent the last fifteen minutes letting Jeremy know how kind it was of them to give someone fresh out of prison, like me, a job. To his credit, Jeremy did not hold this against me. He said he admired my work ethic and that my past was just that…the past. He did let me know that we should inform the current owners, which we did. And they had no problems with keeping me on board either. Not only did they keep me on board, they offered me the General Manager position at the gym in which I was already working, as they were about to open a second location.

I felt like I had just won the lottery. This is exactly what I had hoped for…an opportunity. I knew that if I could just get my foot in the door somewhere, I would be able to make the best of the situation. And it happened. Not the way I expected, but that's life. Our plans rarely work out like we draw them up, but if we remain diligent, we can always get to where we want to be.

The owners knew that I was a personal trainer, but wanted me to gain some hands-on experience as well. They arranged for me to go on the road and learn from Jeremy for the next one hundred and twenty days. I couldn't wait. I gave my notice at the factory the next day, and within two weeks Jeremy and I hit the road together consulting with different gyms. I learned very quickly that Jeremy is a wealth of knowledge. He is a certified genius when it comes to the fitness industry. If you don't believe me, just ask him. I felt like I earned my Master's Degree in those one hundred and twenty days.

We started early and finished late. Jeremy was always teaching. I learned about new equipment, new trends, new marketing techniques, new sales approaches, how to deal with different personalities in the industry and every in and out of the business that goes on behind the scenes. At the end of my time with Jeremy, I actually felt overqualified to run a gym. Please don't interpret that last line as egotistical. It's meant to be more of a compliment to Jeremy than anything else.

The new location opened for business, and Jeremy and I said our goodbyes, although we would keep in touch and talk now and then. I went on to manage the gym for a year and a half, all the while continuing my education as well. I earned the title of Master Trainer through the National Federation of Professional Trainers (NFPT), the same organization I earned my original certification from in prison. In fact, I became a State Representative for NFPT. I studied and became as knowledgeable as I possibly could on everything from nutrition to cardio to resistance training. I eventually made enough of a name for myself that I applied and was accepted to become one of their Subject Matter Experts.

I was flown to Florida to meet with and sit on a board with other experts. This was somewhat intimidating for me. All of the others were formally trained for years to be as knowledgeable as they were. Besides the certification programs I had completed, my knowledge came from knowing all of the NFPT manuals inside and out. I studied them like my life depended on it, and it paid off. When it was time for me to speak at this meeting, I actually sounded like I knew what I was talking about…because I did. I knew the organization. I knew the subject matter. And I knew my audience. Having a handle on those three ingredients is a recipe for success.

The highlight of that trip was meeting Ron Clark, the founder and CEO of NFPT. As I shook hands with him and talked, I couldn't help but think back to taking his entry-level exam in prison three short years before. Now I was one of his Subject Matter Experts. It was a reminder that it doesn't matter from where you start…we all have the same opportunity to finish strong.

Not too much further into the future, a new gym was generating a lot of buzz in the area. Body Renew Fitness was getting ready to open. And the owner was going to be none other than my old pal, Jeremy. He and I went out to celebrate his new business venture, and after catching up for a while the conversation turned to career opportunities. The writing was on the wall that I had climbed as high as I was going to at the gym where I currently was. There was no more room for advancement. I asked Jeremy if he thought there would be any room for growth at his establishment. He told me that he thought there could be, but he had already hired a General Manager. If I wanted to come on board, I would have to start as a personal trainer and work my way up from there.

Trying to look at the switch from a 'big picture' point of view, I gave my notice and came to work for Jeremy as one of his trainers. Over the next three years, I worked my way up from personal trainer to Assistant Manager, all the way to General Manager. Then came the moment I had been waiting for. Jeremy called me into his office and offered to make me a partner. This was *that* moment I had worked so hard for. It was the moment I thought at times I would never see. It was that moment I sometimes thought I wasn't good enough for. But I never stopped. Sure, I had my doubts, but the important thing was that I never acted on any of them. In the end, my faith overshadowed my doubts, and I eventually earned what I so desperately wanted. I just wish Juice could have been there to enjoy the moment with me.

This was a different goal than my original one of wanting to be a gangster and a respected dealer. For the first time, I truly believed in what I was doing. I was actually making a difference in the world…in a positive way this time. And that's what I wanted. After all the pain and suffering I'd either seen or caused in my life, it was time for a change. It was time to start helping others instead of tearing them down. It was time to take ownership of my life and encourage others to do the same.

I would never have been successful without the help of a lot of good people in my life along the way. I will never forget what they have done and continue to do for me. God has seen me through a lot in my life and has given me much to be thankful for. But what I think I'm most thankful for are my family and friends who have supported me through this crazy journey.

And the exciting part is that this isn't the end. It's only the beginning. It's time for new goals and continued growth. After years of forging harmful prescriptions, please allow me to prescribe some helpful ones for you in the next chapter.

Life Prescriptions

Okay, so here we are...the moment of truth. It's time for me to recap the life prescriptions that enabled me to change my life. You're probably expecting the latest and greatest step-by-step system to instantly make all your dreams a reality. Well, I've got good news and bad news. The bad news is that, to my knowledge, no such overnight success formula exists. The good news is that making your dreams a reality isn't as complicated or unattainable as you may think. It's actually quite simple. Notice I said simple, not *easy.*

First and foremost, you must take personal responsibility for your current position in life. Regardless of how you arrived there, you need to take ownership of your life and decide that if you want something different, it's up to you and only you to make that happen. Once you take personal responsibility, which is a huge accomplishment most people never achieve, you can begin the journey of slowly but surely changing your dreams into your reality through the three-pronged approach exemplified in my story.

Most importantly, the first prong, I was introduced to

and developed a relationship with God. The experience of connecting with something greater than myself humbled my ego while simultaneously giving me the strength to make the necessary changes to become a better person, as well as live a healthier life.

Then, through the second prong, I addressed my health by getting clean, slowly increasing my physical activity and improving my overall diet. Remember that I didn't jump right into a high-intensity exercise routine or go on a starvation diet to make these changes. I sought out a mentor in this area who slowly introduced and taught me the fundamentals of exercise and nutrition.

Last but definitely not least, the third prong…I invested time, effort, and resources in educating myself on the areas necessary to achieve my goals. Whether that is a certification program like NFPT or one of the hundreds of personal development books on the market. Your mind is like any other muscle, you either use it or lose it.

But as important as this three-pronged approach is, please remember one thing. It all starts with a single moment. It begins with the moment you make a choice that you want to change the way you're living your life. And it's not just making that choice. It's also critical that you *believe* in the choice you're making. If you make a choice to change your life, but don't really believe it can happen…odds are that it probably won't. You must truly believe that you can change before you will ever see the actual transition occur. It's all about personal accountability. You believe…you blossom. If you doubt…you're done.

Just remember we all have obstacles to overcome. That's life, no excuses. But if I can go from being a high school dropout with six felony convictions, being addicted to pills and being more than one hundred pounds overweight to being an in-shape, motivated, successful business owner, author and speaker, let's be honest…the sky is pretty much the limit for most anyone else. Hopefully, you're in a better starting place than I was (and I sincerely hope you are), or you're currently traveling down the same destructive road that I did, but just remember the U turn to success is *always* waiting for you. It's just a matter of turning that steering wheel, stepping on the gas pedal and never looking back. We can and should learn from our past, but we should never dwell there. The future demands more of our focus than the past. That's why the windshield on your car is bigger than your rearview mirror.

So there you have it, the simple but not always easy Life Prescriptions that enabled me to turn my dreams into my reality. Remember that this is not an instant gratification system. It took me ten years of consistently applying these principles to turn my life around, and I'm still a work in progress. That being said, I greatly appreciate you allowing me to share my journey with you, and hope that it has a positive impact on your own. Oh, and if you happen to find that overnight success formula, please be sure to let me know because I know just the guy to *forge*…I mean *write* the prescription.

About The Author

Matthew D. Hirschberg, personal trainer, business owner, motivational speaker, and author, enjoys sharing his life story and the lessons he has learned along the way. Matt is currently the Chief Operations Officer of Body Renew Fitness and a Master Trainer, State Representative and Subject Matter Expert through the National Federation of Professional Trainers. He also holds separate  certifications through the National Academy of Sports Medicine, CrossFit, TRX and ViPR. Once he decided to take personal responsibility for his life and the poor decisions of his past, Matt focused on his health, business acumen and his faith. Since then, he has been able to build a new life on the foundation of his old one.

From dropping out of high school to a life of crime and drugs, to a four-year stint in a federal prison, to his battle with obesity, he has overcome much and inspired others along the way. For the first time ever, Matt opens up and shares his untold story of how he overcame adversity and turned his life around. In his free time Matt enjoys hiking, travel and community outreach in the Shenandoah Valley of Virginia where he currently resides.